T0190596

THE NOVELIST'S LEXICON

THE NOVELIST'S LEXICON

WRITERS ON THE WORDS
THAT DEFINE THEIR WORK

EDITED BY VILLA GILLET/LE MONDE

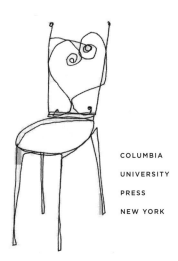

COLUMBIA

UNIVERSITY

PRESS

NEW YORK

Columbia University Press
Publishers Since 1893
New York   Chichester, West Sussex

Lexique nomade copyright © 2008 Villa Gillet, published by Christian Bourgois éditeur

Translation copyright © 2011 Columbia University Press.
All rights reserved

Library of Congress Cataloging-in-Publication Data
Lexique nomade. English
The novelist's lexicon : writers on the words that define their work / edited by Villa Gillet.
  p. cm.
Translation of: Lexique nomade [a collection of short meditations by contemporary novelists at the 3rd Assises internationales du roman]
Includes index.
ISBN 978-0-231-15080-4 (cloth : alk. paper) — ISBN 978-0-231-52169-7 (ebook)
1. Fiction—Technique—Congresses. 2. Fiction—Authorship—Congresses.
I. Villa Gillet (Association) II. Assises internationales du roman (3rd : 2009 : Lyon, France) III. Title.

PN3365.L48   2009
808.3—dc22   2009038310

Columbia University Press books are printed on permanent and durable acid-free paper.
This book is printed on paper with recycled content.
Printed in the United States of America
c 10 9 8 7 6 5 4 3 2 1

Artwork by Lisa Force / Designed by Lisa Hamm

References to Internet Web sites (URLs) were accurate at the time of writing. Neither the author nor Columbia University Press is responsible for URLs that may have expired or changed since the manuscript was prepared.

CONTENTS

FOREWORD xi

PREFACE xiii

A

ADUMBRATED | RICK MOODY 1

ALETHERATURE | HÉLÈNE CIXOUS 2

AMEN | ZERUYA SHALEV 4

ANONYMITY | COLUM MCCANN 4

AUTOFICTION | PHILIPPE VILAIN 5

AVAILABLE | LYONEL TROUILLOT 7

AWARENESS OF BANALITY | DIMITRI VERHULST 8

B

BALAGAN | ETGAR KERET 10

THE BANANA REPUBLIC OF LETTERS | CHLOÉ DELAUME 11

BEAUTY | ROBERT DESSAIX 12

BILDUNGSROMAN | UPAMANYU CHATTERJEE 13

BRETON | CHRISTOPHE HONORÉ 14

BRICOLEUR | MONIKA FAGERHOLM 15

C

CATIN | JACQUES HENRIC 17

CHAFF | AYERDHAL 18

CINDERELLA | ERIC REINHARDT 19

CREATURE | ALISSA YORK 23

CUNNILINGUS | RIKKI DUCORNET 24

D

DISAPPOINTMENT | NELLY ARCAN 26

DISCIPLINE | ENRIQUE VILA-MATAS 28

DREAM | DANY LAFERRIÈRE 29

E

ÉCHAPPÉE | MARIE DESPLECHIN 31

EVOLUTION | KAREN CONNELLY 32

F

FAIRE | CHRISTINE ANGOT 34

FILLE | ALAIN FLEISCHER 35

FURNITURE | JONATHAN LETHEM 37

H

HAPPINESS | WEI-WEI 38

HARMONY AND | HWANG SOK-YONG 40
   RECONCILIATION

HEDONISM | ADAM THIRLWELL   42

HERETIC | ANDRÉ BRINK   43

HONESTY | PETER STAMM   45

I

"I" | RACHID EL DAIF   46

IDENTITIES | NURUDDIN FARAH   47

WISE IMAGINATION | PASCAL MERCIER   49

INDIA | TARUN J. TEJPAL   49

INSOMNIA | LUDMILA ULITSKAYA   50

ISLAND | ERRI DE LUCA   53

L

TO LAST | GIUSEPPE CULICCHIA   55

LAUGHTER | TARIQ ALI   56

LIES | ADRIAAN VAN DIS   58

LOYALTY | DUONG THU HUONG   63

M

MARIQUITA | JAMES CAÑÓN   65

THE MEANING OF A WORD . . . | KIRSTY GUNN   67

THE STROLLING MIRROR | RODRIGO FRESÁN   67

N

NO | OLIVIA ROSENTHAL   70

NO WHY | YANNICK HAENEL   73

NOMAD | ELIF SHAFAK   74

THE NOVEL AS WEB | A. S. BYATT   76

NOVEL/LIFE | JAMES MEEK   77

WHAT IS THE NOVEL? | ALAA EL ASWANY   78

NOVICE | NICOLAS FARGUES   80

P

PARALIPOMENA | LYDIE SALVAYRE   81

PATHOS | ALBERTO GARLINI   83

PHANTOM | YING CHEN   84

PHYSICAL | LUC LANG   85

~~PLAGUE~~ | DAVID PEACE   87

(THE) PRESENT | JEAN-YVES CENDREY   87

R

"REAL" | PHILIPPE FOREST   90

THE REAL | NICOLE MALINCONI   91

(HOLY) RUSSIA | GENEVIÈVE BRISAC   93

S

A SUCCESSFUL SENTENCE | GILA LUSTIGER   95

SHADOW | ELISABETTA RASY   96

SIGNED D.C. | DENNIS COOPER   98

SILENCE | DAVID ALBAHARI   99

THE DEPOPULATED SKIES | THOMAS JONIGK   100

SUFFERING | FATOS KONGOLI   102

T

TERROIR | ANNIE PROULX   104

U

UN- | JONAS HASSEN KHEMIRI 106

UNKNOWABLE | DANIEL MENDELSOHN 108

THE UNREAL | ARTHUR JAPIN 109

W

WAITING/ATTENTION | ANNE WEBER 112

WOMAN | BENOÎTE GROULT 113

THE WORD _WORD_ | LESLIE KAPLAN 114

"WORDS, WORDS, WORDS" | PÉTER ESTERHÁZY 116

WORK | RAFAEL CHIRBES 117

Y

YUSUF | SUHAYL SAADI 120

Z

ZORBY | JAMES FLINT 122

CONTRIBUTORS 125

INDEX 143

FOREWORD: THE COURAGE OF WORDS

THE UNIVERSE of a novel opens a world for us. The world slips in and inhabits the book. It slips inside the book in its own way because novelists each have their own way of summoning it with their words, emotions, sensations, the things they know and don't know, what they are and what others are; they summon what is, though they may not always know what it's all about. The novelist uses words, though words also use the novelist in order to make reality bear a likeness to them, unless the opposite is true. In a novel words and reality react against one another until they find a good fit. They start resonating. They create sentences and rhythms. They welcome and reject one another. They seek one another out. This is the work of the imagination. The novelist ventures out into words. Words venture out into the world. Without the courage for this adventure there would be no novel. The novelist gives courage to words. If the novelist fails to take the gamble, the gamble of language that can never be controlled, literature will fail to respond to him; and if words fail to take the gamble of literature, the world will not inhabit them. Words expose us because they do not belong to us. They have migrated from mouth to mouth, from book to book. They carry a memory older than ours. They are more knowledgeable than we are. But they let us make use of them provided we make them come alive, that is, provided we give them their freedom back, for they are so often the prisoners of usage and convention.

Each page of this nomadic lexicon is a moment of freedom for them. We asked each novelist to choose a key word that opens the doors to his work. But, as everyone knows, a work never surrenders its keys, because its doors remain unlocked at all times; whether we push them open depends solely on us. It is therefore probable that the key each novelist offers us is the key that puts us to the test of words, for words are so good at traveling inside one another, so good at crossing all frontiers, inasmuch as their meanderings create shifting territories, wide-open fields in which to lose one's keys.

Guy Walter
Director, Villa Gillet
Translated by Catherine Temerson

PREFACE: APT WORDS

ONE WORD, just one. . . . It can seem like a cruel exercise. Doesn't the novelist bathe in words all day long? Doesn't he have at least a thousand verbs and a thousand adjectives at the tip of his pen?

The contributors to this book played the game, aware that this was not a beauty contest. They were not asked to comment on their favorite word but on the word that best provides an introduction to their work.

Olivia Rosenthal chose the word *no*. She always answers no; it's a principle with her, even if it can be discussed later on. No, no, and no. A joyous refusal, full of energy, and final. Her contribution succeeds in introducing us to the work . . . of Thomas Bernhard, a writer she much admires. And so it goes, one thing leading to another; that's how this book moves forward, with no prior agreement among the authors, one author's word referring to another's.

Jonas Hassen Khemiri chose *o,* the prefix expressing a negative in Swedish (*un* in English). Another way of saying no. Dany Laferrière talks to us about *dream,* Nicole Malinconi about the *real,* and Arthur Japin about the *unreal.* The latter explains why the novelist is wrong to want to create lifelike characters, for the reader can only identify with the extraordinary. So here we are again, back in Dany Laferrière's dream, which brings us to *insomnia,* the word chosen by Ludmila Oulitskaya, but also to the *real* of Nicole Malinconi (not to be confused with reality, which is just a poor relative of the real).

Nicolas Fargues offers us *novice,* which is as good a way as any of saying something fundamental: "Watch out for words that strike a pose." Any one of the contributors to this book would willingly add his signature to the next sentence: "But do let your memory and your instincts flow—let the aptest words, the words that resemble you most closely, come of their own accord."

Yes, a novelist rings true when he uses the *aptest* words. Readers can't be fooled.

Robert Solé
Le Monde
Translated by Catherine Temerson

THE NOVELIST'S LEXICON

A

ADUMBRATED | RICK MOODY

Adjective, a partial and incomplete definition herewith because a complete definition would be going too far and giving too much away; *adumbrated,* suggestive, allusive, as in a chalk mark around a fallen body, a body at a crime scene; the precise demarcation of the interrelation between crime and criminal, at the time, impossible to render; *adumbrated,* containing *umbra,* from the Latin for *shadow,* pertaining to all things *shadowy*; a spectacularly good word, *shadow,* which in turn incompletely summons the Greek *skotos,* darkness, such that *adumbrated* alludes to, contains, surfeits, intimates concealment in darkness, and though *what is written* is *written* so as to cast a light, to make *lucid* or *radiant,* the nature of this scripted, sketched-out beginning is often such that what is revealed is also left in half-light, in *penumbra*; *shadow,* a colorless cell or empty membrane, a toneless tonality, unless the tonality is of darkness, which has no tone; *adumbrated,* containing also *umbrage,* a state of *annoyance,* so that *penumbra,* especially in the thick, shady branches of a tree, is next door to *annoyance,* and even *obsolescence;* if literature gives light, part of its brief, its mission, is also annoyance, annoyance with oversimplifications, annoyance with excesses of light, with the false dependability of what is, without failing to suggest, though insubstantially and partially, what is *not.*

ALETHERATURE | HÉLÈNE CIXOUS

Who's there? No one knows, no one will ever know who or what will have already begun, before us, in the dark. We are stopped. There's a presentiment. A *touch of summer* [rayonnement d'été] reaches us. Or else *of having been* [d'avoir été]. Of having already been there.—What then?—The memory is lost. But that's where I'm going. Behind the screen, moving back toward the truth whose scent-of-cherries-on-the-table I have picked up, I see: beside the road where, having fled the colloquia and universities, my son and I have just stopped, I see, and it's a surprise in this deserted autumn, two populated trees. In one a choir of a thousand birds greets the dawn. In the other ten thousand butterflies of the same kind are making their dream honey. Am I high up in Algiers? Then surely these trees are ficuses. I will tell my friend Derrida. I raise my head. They are acacias! The meager acacias of the rue d'Alésia that saw Jean Genet pass by. I lower my eyes; what do I see? Where the road was now a rapid river flows.

Behind my back as well the water rises; it can't be denied. It is the Flood. I had just enough time to grab my cell phone lying on the ground. Already the water surrounds us. My son and I are standing on a bank without an ark. I call J.D. He, too, is surrounded by the water over there.—Where are you? I say—Near General Er, he tells me.—General Er? Where's that? Do you know General Er? I asked my son, who knows everything. And this water that is slowly invading the world? It then occurs to me that this water which invades and separates, slow, nonviolent, inexorable, is none other than *the Lethe*! Yes, yes it's Lethe! So, this is it, the thing, the name that comes to the sacred lips of King Hamlet the Ghost when he addresses his son Hamlet warily, saying: "It is I, Hamlet, are you listening to me? Or are you floating, distracted, like *the fat weed that rots itself in ease on Lethe's wharf*? On which side of Lethe are you? Are you sleeping? Or are you apt to follow me *over to the side of Aletherature*: if you follow me, I will tell you all the secrets that cannot be revealed. Except in dreams."

Clearly literature is never where you think. It is not in the story. It is in the elbows of the sentences. In the ferry, behind the window. It is guarded, dissimulated behind a piece of canvas, disseminated in the idiom, in the trees of the idiom. They hold out their naïve arms, which have a passion for birds, so as to tell us the secret that they sense I may or may not untangle.

TRANSLATED FROM THE FRENCH BY PEGGY KAMUF

AMEN | ZERUYA SHALEV

The word *amen*, which found its way from Judaism into Christianity and Islam, crossing cultures and continents, borders and chasms, is in fact an acronym of the Hebrew phrase "el melech ne'eman." Spoken in response to a blessing, it means: the words of the blessing are true and may they come to pass. It is a succinct and restrained expression of hope and faith, a prayer and a wish.

Walking on an unfamiliar street in a foreign country, a foreign city, where an incomprehensible language is spoken and I suddenly hear that ancient Hebrew word drifting out of the windows of a church, I feel the warmth of home, remembering in amazement that it was from here that the message of redemption went forth into the world, from my small country on the western edge of Asia, a country that has known so much suffering and so many reversals.

Since that word is so universal, it symbolizes for me, much as literature does, everything that we, all of humanity, have in common despite the differences in our way of thinking, in our faith, and our inner and outer landscapes, the living, quivering hope of every human being for forgiveness, salvation, mercy. And so I think that even the very fact of its existence is comforting, although all our wishes may not come true.

TRANSLATED FROM THE HEBREW BY SONDRA SILVERSTON

ANONYMITY | COLUM MCCANN

That which should not be silenced. The story that needs to be told. The story that seldom gets told. The story that tells other stories. The part of the world that is left dusty. The part of the world that is ignored. The part of the world necessary to the written word. The character of the person indispensable to the story, to the world, to the word.

Adjective, noun, verb, curse, gracenote.

AUTOFICTION | PHILIPPE VILAIN

Noun—from *auto* (*biography*) and *fiction* DIDACT. Term invented and defined in 1977 by Serge Doubrovsky upon publication of his novel entitled *Fils* (Son): "Fiction, made up of events and facts that are strictly real." Added to this definition are two fundamental clauses: (1) *nominal* (autofiction requires homonymy among its author, narrator, and character; this clause distinguishes autofiction from the autobiographical novel, in which the author bestows a borrowed name upon a character); (2) *generic* (autofiction plays on its generic ambiguity, on its "contradictory pact," on presenting itself as both absolutely referential, since it is subject to a principle of factual exactitude, and nonreferential, since by claiming to be a novel it attests to [indicates, announces] its entrance into fiction). To confuse the world, certain theoreticians have felt the need to refine the definition or, like Philippe Lejeune, to distinguish between "referential autofiction" and "fictional autofiction." Currently practitioners of autofiction from two [both] camps are taking part in acerbic verbal jousting for the monopoly of the Holy Grail: the Purists, respectful of the Doubrovskyan bible, and the Infidels, who see autofiction as a simple resurgence of the autobiographical novel. Beyond that, the Manichaeism that autofiction inspires, the adherence and rejection it encounters, the theoretical debate it incites should point up its dazzling arrival on the contemporary literary landscape. It is possible that the singularity of autofiction has to do with its indefinable character or, more precisely, with the fact that since its creation its definition has been a matter of constant questioning, the object of a recurrent attempt to make it more precise. **BY EXT**. The *Doubrovskyan* sense of the word has nevertheless shifted over the past several years. The term, which has now entered the vernacular, refers to everything and its opposite. Don't we say: "What is this thing, autofiction, really?" ["C'est quoi ce truc, l'autofiction, au juste?"] Following fashion, we call "autofiction" just about everything that has to do with autobiography generally; hence the polysemic expression: "Ah, so it's autofiction!" (*vulg.* "C'mon, you liar, what is this, a bunch of autofiction?")—which, it must be underscored, is not very valorizing. People also say "faire de l'autofiction" (doing autofiction) like "faire du cheval" (riding a horse) or "faire ses courses" (going shopping), no doubt to signify that this genre is a sport like any other, that it is practiced more than it is intellectualized. **BY EXT. OF THE EXT**. It would be suicidal to link oneself to a practitioner of autofiction, who, according to knowledgeable scholars in textual genetics, has the particularity of being deeply narcissistic, immodest, and amoral. Are these the reasons for which a number of writers whose texts are part of autofiction feel reluctant to assume the genre (or affiliate with it, depending on fashion and circumstances), as has so heroically been assumed by the master Serge Doubrovsky, the incorrigible Christine Angot, the redoubtable Camille Laurens, and myself, the *vilain* (homely) Narcissus.

TRANSLATED FROM THE FRENCH BY JEANINE HERMAN

AVAILABLE | LYONEL TROUILLOT

"People . . . it would be best to know them only when they are available, open . . . at certain pale hours of the night . . . with problems that are simply human, problems of melancholy." I love "melancholy" and, above all, "available." Melancholy, that is a sickness that cures us of many others: smugness, the fear of doubt. It makes us live riskily: word and gesture, silence and action flirting with depression, from a need to engage wholeheartedly.

In a way, melancholy resembles Romanticism, but the resemblance is deceptive because the Romantic—forefather of autofiction (the sorrows of Werther, the sadness of Olympio), convinced of his own importance even in his lamentations—awards himself a diploma in heroism.

Available, but in a simpler way, without the constant examination of one's self. Like that boy who tells the story of his sister's fine capacity for revolt (*The Children of Heroes*). Like that student who strides firmly but modestly toward a freedom that sometimes passes through death (*Bicentenary*). Like that writer—a "public letter writer," let's say—who recounts the love stories of others (*Love Before I Forget*).

Basically, the disquiet that suits me the most as a novelist and human being is the fear of running a deficit of availability.

Available, simply. Without reservation or exploitation.

"If one day people are able to calmly watch the people they love make love, humanity will be the better for it." I love this plan for openness to the rights and beauty of the other's body.

There is enough bread to feed everyone, but children die of hunger. I love this availability that makes the sharing of bread a matter of concern.

We are sometimes so visible that we forget to look. (Being) available: or disappearing . . . the better to see.

TRANSLATED FROM THE FRENCH BY LINDA COVERDALE

AWARENESS OF BANALITY | DIMITRI VERHULST

The chance of readers coming to tell me that they identified with parts of my work is greatest when I have simply talked about myself in an honest way. Don't get me wrong: identification is not necessarily the quality a book should aspire to in order to produce good literature. Please, let literature be as many things as possible. But identification remains a facet that large numbers of readers appreciate. And it is possibly a function, one of the many, of literature: assurance through identification, demonstrating that we share many of our peculiarities with others. That we are unique, but in moderation. That is why I need to write from the ground and never from the pulpit. Being human first, and only then a writer. Shrugging off my prizes and titles when I sit down at my desk. And finding myself uninteresting enough to write about or draw on, because the stories *that* leads to are truer than the stories produced by someone who writes about himself or from his perspective because he considers himself interesting. Perhaps this is a way of thinking up words that identify with their readers.

TRANSLATED FROM THE DUTCH BY DAVID COLMER

B

BALAGAN | ETGAR KERET

Balagan, a word that migrated to the Hebrew language from Yiddish, means "total chaos." But this word is unique because, contrary to the implied negative value the concept has in other languages, the subtext of *balagan* is positive. True, that positiveness is not overt—a bit like a proud parent trying to hide a smile from his mischief-making son—but it is completely there. Yet chaos for a society that is itself full of *balagan* is nothing less than proof of vitality and passion. In a place where people push and shove in line, where children insist on drawing on walls and not on paper, where a briefcase holds stained income tax reports lying between a pastrami sandwich and a piece of graph paper with the beginnings of a poem on it—that's where you'll find human liberty, the liberty that both Yiddish and Hebrew have always held sacred.

The Banana Republic of Letters (BRL) is landlocked inside the Editorial Kingdom and covers an area of 2.2 square kilometers made up of permanent houses and shifting zones. Its altitude is negative, although it includes a hill, and on its summit is the Castle. Its latitude and longitude cannot be determined because of the ephemeral nature of many of its domains, which vanish every time the surveyors arrive. Its population density is 20,666 inhabitants per square kilometer, and its economic model takes inspiration from the handbook of corruption and Palatine economics. By conducting an expansionist policy, in recent decades the BRL has absorbed a number of neighboring states, such as Ethicsistan or the Laboratories of the East. As one of the presidents of the regime emphasized, "The frontiers of the Banana Republic of Letters will break off beyond this world." Hence BRL colonies regularly settle on the Internet, where they flourish and multiply. Monitored by Amnesty International for several years, the BRL is famous for its two national holidays, including its Great September Sacrifice, which slanders, tortures, and crucifies human beings every autumn for the greater pleasure of the public and the participants. The BRL's citizens worship Commerce and the Spectacular. Their customs, habits, and practices reflect a certain West where polar bears are not feared. Though the BRL's existence has been proven at the start of every literary season, its name is not associated with a concrete geographical entity but rather with an expression.

TRANSLATED FROM THE FRENCH BY CATHERINE TEMERSON

Beauty is something that happens deep inside us.

Although beauty has only become fashionable again recently and did not exist for most of the inhuman twentieth century, its roots are ancient and tangled. It has been linked to objective criteria (symmetrical faces; bodies good for breeding; landscapes suggestive of fecundity). It has also been considered a subjective response to the world. (If I think "Non, je ne regrette rien," sung by Piaf, is more beautiful than Beethoven's Ninth Symphony, then it is; if I think Depardieu is more handsome than Johnny Depp, then he is—it's personal.)

These points of view omit an essential, shared element. We say "How beautiful!" when what we see or hear "embellishes" us, when it enriches our sense of being at root whole, reconfiguring all the shards in our inner kaleidoscope—our deepest and also most banal memories, desires, fears—to make us feel at root whole, intact, unique, real despite everything. It recomposes me.

This feeling is particularly strong when there is tension in the new pattern, a force that seems to twist the soul: calm and violence, darkness and light, maleness and femininity. It's ravishingly pleasurable.

Our soul is also twisted by the desire to hang on to what is beautiful, while knowing that at any moment we must let go. The pleasure is always imbued with a sense of bereavement. We always want to experience the beautiful—see a beloved face; hear a beautiful piece of music—one more time. We can't possess it; we can only wonder at it.

Consequently for the immoralist beauty and goodness are the same thing. For the moralist beauty is a temptation unless it is divine.

Beauty is an act of transfiguration, a sudden paraphrasing of our most authentic sensibilities.

BILDUNGSROMAN | UPAMANYU CHATTERJEE

Hate traveling, hate packing and the dislocation, the airport, and the damned nine-hour flight, the terrible food in the plane, the weirdo behind me who won't let me push back my seat, Passport Control sniffing my passport because it smells of naphthalene balls from my coat while I try to explain that in torrid tropical Bombay one doesn't *wear* coats. Will drink like a European and arrive in Lyon with a hangover. Hate meeting people. Will want to start smoking again but won't find Wills Navy Cut anywhere and will therefore smoke brands that I don't want to touch. Hate the weather, rain, and a cold wind that takes your breath away. Wrong clothes, dry skin, and how I hate tea bags, they were never meant for Darjeeling.

Why do you write in English. Is it to earn dollars. Why don't you write like R. K. Narayan. Why don't you write in Sanskrit. Why don't you go back to the Vedas. Why don't you write like Roberto Calasso. Why do you deny the autobiographical in your oeuvre. What caste are you. When did you last spit on someone whose shadow touched you. Do you follow Brahma or Brahman. Do you travel to work on an elephant. Do you avoid garlic on Thursdays.

Long pause.

Hey, Ram, what the hell is Bildungsroman? bordello

And yet, and yet, accept all invitations and globe-trot every year.

BRETON | CHRISTOPHE HONORÉ

References to Brittany in world literature are very restrained and inexplicably scarce. Probably a goodly number of published writers have never witnessed the circling will-o'-the-wisps near Brennilis running between the hedges, setting fire to a tree here, a village there. Let me inform those writers that Brittany is a land of wise minds who are fully aware that a dead person is a being who still exists in another shape or state: menhir; dog; voices of wandering souls in the cold hell of the wind. Contact between the dead and the living is the main activity of this supposedly austere people, yet their prime quality is cunning. Indeed, Bretons spend their lives on the lookout for mysterious signs which, as Anatole Le Braz explained, "are like a shadow, projected ahead, of what is bound to happen." Let me add that if the mysterious signs announce death, the person to whom the sign appears is rarely the one threatened by death. You'll admit that such a people—both curious about death's extraordinary guises and always quick to warn their fellow man of his death espied— possess two of the essential virtues expected of a writer. At least for the writer-filmmaker that I am, who imagines himself proudly desecrating reality through cinema and poisoning himself, through literature, with the powers of death. Otherwise, objectively speaking, I admit that Bretons are the worst marine poets in the world. Even Tristan Corbière is hopeless at sea poems.

TRANSLATED FROM THE FRENCH BY CATHERINE TEMERSON

BRICOLEUR | MONIKA FAGERHOLM

For me I choose the word *bricoleur* for two reasons. First, it is one of my favorite French words, although I don't know exactly what it means; it has a nice "clickering" sound to it and a sense of movement, of combination and constructing.... Of course, something of the meaning I can grasp since I do know some French, but no, I am not on my way to the bookshelf to find a dictionary to find out more. I don't want a dictionary. I want to fill in the gaps with my own intuition and imagination, to create.... In moments of daring I would like to state: I want to create meaning, write something I did not know that I knew already. Second, in her biography about James Joyce's daughter, Lucia, who had a short career as a modern dancer and choreographer in Paris in the thirties, Carol Loeb Schloss writes the following seductive sentences: "She was a sort of *bricoleur,* someone dancing with emotional and cultural structures, swindling authority, violating boundaries, reworking and transgressing an identification at the very moment it was being constituted. She was a young girl who, amid the collective judgment that she was 'wonderfully sweet,' was privately engaged in stealing fire. . . ." After reading that, the question poses itself: Who would NOT want to be like that? As a writer, too, I mean? Sweet but dangerous, subversive. . . . However, at the same time, reading this passage and thinking about my image of Lucia as it emerges from this same biography, I am suddenly not all that sure I unconditionally believe it. Big, abstract words around a person who might also have been just someone restless and confused; who went looking for a "platform" to work and be from but did not find it, despite all the dance, despite all the talent in the world. What I mean is that these words say a lot about what we would so much *like* to see. . . . So, then, this has to be included in *my* definition: all the doubt, the sense of gaps not to be abridged, of unworthiness and shame. But to, while writing, not turn one's back on them, pretend they don't exist, but move with them, swiftly, as a silverfish (Lucia J. in her most famous dance costume, by the way).

C

CATIN | JACQUES HENRIC

Catin, noun (mid-16th cen.): an affectionate diminutive of Catherine (diminutive Cathy). From the Latin *Katerina* of Alexandria, virgin martyr; from the Greek *katheros,* "pure." The pejorative sense, meaning "a woman of loose morals," has replaced the earlier sense.[1]

I explained in *Comme si notre amour était une ordure*[2] (Stock) that even as a child my first great love was the *catin* (in the secondary sense) in the little village in the Beauce where I lived. For me, from the first, the unacceptable was at the very heart of passion, of love, of sex. How, then, in my writing, in my life, could I possibly deal with those whom Baudelaire referred to as "les orduriers," otherwise known as the bleating, bleeding-heart advocates of harmony between the sexes. "God is the most prostituted being," declared the

....

1. An archaic word for a prostitute analogous to "trollop" or "harlot."
2. As though our love were shit.

very Christian author of *Les Fleurs du mal*. Did he also think of those devout handmaidens of the Almighty, the "pure" (*catins* in the primary sense), these women of nothingness "capable of God"?[3] Good News (bad for many and for "les orduriers" in particular), though a poet who held to "pure Catholic doctrine" was not the only one to proclaim it. One of the philosophers of the Age of Enlightenment, Diderot, preceded him and a Jewish doctor, the puritan Sigmund Freud, who exacerbate the message. And which, down the centuries, others, writers—I speak of the best of them, those whom Kierkegaard called "eroticians," and women, especially the women—the best of them, by which I mean the "pure" (taking the meaning that suits). Incidentally, have you ever, like the narrator of *À la recherche du temps perdu* embarking "on the sleep" of Albertine (a *catin*; choose a connotation), spent hours watching a woman as she sleeps, that mass of darkness shot through with violent bursts of light?

TRANSLATED FROM THE FRENCH BY FRANK WYNNE

CHAFF | AYERDHAL

To be chaff, page after page, book after book, is to frolic, scythe in hand, in the field of perfectly upright, perfectly aligned, perfectly patented words that the wheat merchants sell us in the form of telegenically marketed masturbation, and to oppose the ready-to-think in all its varieties.

TRANSLATED FROM THE FRENCH BY ARTHUR GOLDHAMMER

---

3. Saint Augustine's concept that "the soul is capable of God."

CINDERELLA | ERIC REINHARDT

I spent a good deal of the autumn of 2004 both at the Opéra National de Paris, watching the choreographer Angelin Preljocaj create his ballet *Medea,* and on the terrace of a café at the Palais-Royal, the Nemours, where some mysterious predilection drew me each day. I would go there as if spurred by some clarification, the promise of a solution or of a new beginning, and this sense was amplified by the atmosphere of autumn, the season of possibility. When I was in the opera house, sheltered within the warm air of the studio, beneath the building's cupola, there in an utterly secluded place, I was at once fleeing myself and trying to find myself. Preljocaj was amazed to see me frenetically scribbling at his side for hours. I told him: "I come here to watch you create and above all to write." I needed to reestablish myself in writing even though no book had yet come into my head, and seeing him work, watching the dancers, absorbing their energy, letting their energy infect me would set sentences off in me. And then in the evening, or mornings before going into the Opéra building, I would sit down at a table at the Nemours, where, with freedom and the luck of lengthy reverie, a book might perhaps take shape. I had only the vaguest intention for this book, which was actually, to quote Ingeborg Bachmann, to "set down myself at the present moment."

I wanted to write a book that would say who I am. I needed to express through language, and to elucidate through a form, some of my most precious sensations. I wanted to elaborate a poetic art that would lay out the reasons—profound and anchored in a particular relation to reality—why the books I have written are written this way and not another. I wanted to talk about literary determinism. We can only write what we write the way we write them. Why? I felt that it had to do mainly with my relation to time, and particularly to the present, and consequently to the importance of sentient experience, of sensation, of atmospheres, of things suggested. Thus the influence of Mallarmé in my approach to literature, or of André Breton, which would be undetectable given the nature of my novels. That this empire of the present felt like a refuge is largely explained by the terror I have always felt at social reality, at business and the world of work. Childhood traumas over a father humiliated, and the certainty that I, too, would be in my turn, led me to invent an array of ploys, the spell as a means to evade fear, and thus the power of magic, of grace, of love. The queen-woman's place in my imagination. The question of social segregation. To attain some other realm, to wish for a fissure in reality, as in *The Hole* or *Brigadoon*, two major films I wanted to discuss. To be one of the elect. To break out of one's social status, one's condition; to invent, to be liberated from oneself, to be acknowledged as unique. To have faith, to believe in it, to believe in oneself, to sustain relations with the world that are not only relations of fear, of defiance, of anxiety, of obedience. How autumn gradually came to be a central phenomenon through which I experience my own existence, with a perspective of its end result. It actually takes having a serious problem with reality to lay such importance, an excessive importance, smacking of pathology, on a season, autumn. And I wanted to recount it in a book and through a form, recount it as a thing belonging to me alone, that fundamental importance of autumn. I wanted to talk about my wife, to describe her, to explore her mystery, to match in sentences the potency of her aura, recount the arch of her foot and my love for her. I'm moving fast, but I go on long and above all it's clear that this thing is taking off in all directions. And it's easy to see that there is not a chance of making a book out of so many loose, disparate marbles clashing, in no imaginable pattern, a disorder, a busy collection, a melody of echoes that might have soothed me for a long while yet. These marbles, these words, these images, these attractions— something was missing to make sense out of their flashes and to put together the conceptual armature of a novel. I felt that something was out there to be found. All that was missing was the key word a person needs who wants to define himself to himself right now.

And one autumn evening it came to the terrace of that café at the Palais-Royal. That mysterious predilection was drawing me daily across that particular point in the geography of Paris toward the unveiling of my book. And one night I saw it, it came to me, it was granted me by way of an epiphany. I understood what fascination that esplanade had been working on my imagination; artist Jean-Michel Othoniel's magical Métro entrance made of glass beads I saw that evening as an elegant carriage. I saw the Palais-Royal esplanade that evening as a ballroom. The cluster lights of the lampposts, their dark cast-iron bases vanishing in the dimness, I saw as chandeliers. I understood that autumn was not merely a temporal span of time but a place, a festive musical place, the locus of an unveiling and of an approval. The motifs of the autumn and of the ballroom overlay one another. And thus I saw Cinderella step down from Othoniel's carriage and move slowly across the esplanade, amid applause, and I understood that her evening would last the length of a season, autumn, bound at its far end by a sort of fateful midnight, and then Mallarmé appeared. I had found the key word for my book, the key that would draw together and give direction to that mass of iron filings of words and images that had been haunting me for months. The key word organized them and caused them to cast reciprocal light on one another, to quote Mallarmé. And the whole thing started to function inside my head like a calculator, a dynamic system for producing connections in limitless profusion; the parameters it set into motion greeted one another and declared their relationship, their curious cousinage: time, midnight, the queen, Mallarmé, the absolute, *Brigadoon,* chores, humiliation, the aspiration to another realm, magic, flight, the shoe, Christian Louboutin, ballerina's toe shoes, grace, dance, Medea, my wife, the arch of a foot, enchantment, the godmother, and so on. Everything came from out of that key word, Cinderella, emerging as obvious. In my novel I named this joyful conceptual agitation the Cinderella System. It is the invisible armature that will support the book's form and its interlaced narrative lines, something between autofiction and pure fiction, fairy tale and realistic story, consolation and forward flight.

TRANSLATED FROM THE FRENCH BY LINDA ASHER

CREATURE | ALISSA YORK

The novel is a creature. As such, it begins with the greatest of mysteries in the smallest of ways. In search of itself, the creature grows. Its development is subtle beyond measure; dividing, multiplying, it differentiates between vessels, chambers, limbs. Every cell knows its purpose: I am gizzard; I am kneecap; I am eye. Soon countless parts take form—fur and scale, fin and wing, tooth and name and mind—the sum of which is but a blind groping toward the whole. The creature is always hungry. Some offerings it accepts as birthright, others it spits back, demanding better. At times it lies quiet. The resulting peace is uneasy, the awful question never far: What if it slips away dreaming and never wakes? There comes a day when it can see, when it lifts its head and looks about. There comes a day when it runs or slinks or swims, or launches itself into the air. It is both common and terribly rare. It takes up space and time well beyond the limits of its own skin, inhabiting paw prints and errant feathers, scent marks and middens and bones. It brightens the blood of its issue. It quickens the flesh of those it chases, or leads in the chase. It alters forever the senses of those who catch sight of it or chance to hear its call. In short, when all goes well—when the stars line up in the heavens—it lives.

Sex absorbed him, of course, but he feared its ambiguous beginnings and vexatious endings—at least until he stumbled upon a well-thumbed book entirely devoted to cunnilingus. It came to him, perhaps not unreasonably, that if he mastered cunnilingus he would not make enemies. When he ended an affair, the woman would feel tender and grateful nonetheless. He learned to be simultaneously admirable and thievish in bed, taking what he wanted and pulling away when more than he bargained for was freely offered. He would fling himself headlong into an encounter before vanishing like an ostrich in a gale. If his many accelerated mistresses would recall the exact moment his ardent visage clouded over, they would also remember how very good he was at cunnilingus and, no matter where they were or with whom, unapologetically roar with laughter. Had the women known about the book, they might have liked him less. Perhaps unfairly. After all, most anyone who is good at something has pored over books—botanists, say, or bakers, roofers. Cunnilingus was his vocation until he died of an undiagnosed bruit.

Remarkable for their numbers, unknown female mourners showed up at his funeral. They looked proprietary because his tongue (and in this way it brings old King Pyrrhus's miraculous toe to mind) had withstood the crematory fire. Looking them over, it occurred to his wife that what she had considered the demonstration of her husband's unique affection (well, she was naïve; everyone said so) was not that at all. Later she found the book at the bottom of a closet. For many months after his death she looked more irritable and perplexed than distraught.

D

DISAPPOINTMENT | NELLY ARCAN

Disappointment is a rat.

Disappointment is what dies last.

It's a tireless rat that bridges the gap between the grandiose space of dream (being everything, doing everything, placing ourselves in the middle of a crowd of others whose only role is that of ecstatic audience) and rickety reality. The rat bridges that gap by carrying his tear gas from one world to the other and by forcing us to let go of our dreams unless we pay the heavy price of insanity.

Disappointment arises in the lull after a wave of efforts has been completed and lasts until hope reappears and engenders a new wave of efforts. In the constant backwash of the surf, we know we will meet our own disappointment, yet we continue to plow ahead because the society of spectacle and publicity in which we live keeps harassing us with methodical, calculated pressure, but our efforts are now imbued with cynicism, that postmodern form of despair.

Disappointment is the endgame of all human experience because, with its merciless materiality and its hard and steadfast boundaries, reality never goes missing. Disappointment is the experience of reality when reality is triumphant. In that sense reality reminds us that our expectations exceed our limits. And disappointment reminds us of their existence. However, we are unable to reconcile ourselves with them because those limits, all around us, are hated, even denied.

When I write I am constantly aware of the imminence of disappointment. From the first words on, I know the verdict has been returned and my writing, as it were, celebrates its inevitability.

Disappointment attaches itself to a wide-open field of objects, but in my own universe it mainly affects the impossible harmony of human desires, in particular those that unite (and break up) men and women. It hovers over the world of sexuality and commercial beauty: prostitution; pornography; female rivalry and narcissism; image tyranny fostered by cosmetic surgery, that ultimate practice of self-rejection. Those paths require relentless efforts to reach their goals: the irreplaceable object of desire symbolized by a young body, offering irresistible sex appeal. And they all run into disappointment as we face the reality of what is fundamentally a replaceable dream body, so easy to reach, like a sublime carrot dangling right in front of our noses. The disappointment doesn't only come from that realization (since we all know it, in theory) but from turning ourselves, over and over, into witnesses to our own disappearance, to our own erasure inside the circle of desire, whether the goal is to triumph over female rivalry or over age.

Disappointment is a rat.

Disappointment is a row of teeth clamped over our dreams of omnipotence produced by a world of hype which mixes together sexual seduction, public acknowledgment, and money, a world which not only invites us to consume but also to prostitute ourselves.

TRANSLATED FROM THE FRENCH BY CATHERINE TEXIER

DISCIPLINE | ENRIQUE VILA-MATAS

Set of norms and canonical dispositions of the novel. I do not believe they should be dismissed as unnecessary or thought of as essentially imposed from without by authoritarians. I adhere to the most ancient tradition, according to which discipline must come from within. It is a mental force emitted by our own genius of the place, the *genius loci* that guides the threads of our narratives, ourselves. The novelist does not free himself by freeing up his impulses or by acting casually and out of control but by subjecting the force of his nature to an idea of the spirit and a dominant project, to a rigid mental code that is able to suppress his wildest freedom and place him in the current downriver of a disciplined and, if possible (thanks to the *genius loci*'s inner designs), moderately sublime life and novel.

TRANSLATED FROM THE SPANISH BY JONATHAN DUNNE

Something happened in my childhood that kept me from ever telling the difference between dream and reality. Living in reality as if it were a dream. There was a little girl who lived at the end of the path just before the curve that leads to the river. I would see her only when she came up my street with her mother. Often I was lying in the gallery studying the crazy ants going about their business in the cracks between the red bricks. I knew that Vava was close by as soon as I started to tremble for no good reason. I'd close my eyes as she went by to avoid being blinded by her radiance. But at night in my dreams she'd come back to me. When I wanted to see her I'd fly right to her doorstep and enter her room through the window. I'd sit in a corner to watch her. She always wore the same yellow dress. She had the high cheekbones of a Mongolian princess and her eyes were so deep that it made me dizzy. In the morning I always woke up feverish and in a sweat. Years later, every time I'd settle down to write, it was her image that appeared before me. And never having actually seen her face, it was even easier to find her back in the writing since I had the same powers there as I used to have in my dreams. When I write I enter the night world, my eyes wide open. And I fly above the houses. I remembered that dreams held me so in thrall that my mother was afraid I would get lost one night in the hallways of sleep. In dreams I had everything. Writing alone has allowed me to find such an immense universe again. I'm comfortable only when I feel I'm floating. And yet I despise dreamlike atmospheres, magic realism, fuzzy artistry. What interests me is not delirium but rather the strict rules that release the freedom of movement I find only in my dreams.

TRANSLATED FROM THE FRENCH BY MARJOLIJN DE JAGER

E

ÉCHAPÉE[1] **| MARIE DESPLECHIN**

Metaphorically, a brief moment or interval. Literally, a space that allows something to be seen; "échappée de vue": a view (afforded by a gap in an obstacle); "échappée de lumière": a shaft of light (shining through an opening). In sports and common usage, a breakaway from the field by one or several competitors (*Dictionnaire historique de la langue française, Le Robert*).

Brief moments or intervals snatched from (the jaws of) life, furtively salted away, liberated from the constant, unremitting, insistent, exhausting demands of the world. Jaunts. Stolen moments. Flight.

A space that allows something to be seen and someone to see, that filters light. Realizations, pleasant or otherwise,

----

1. Noun formed from the past participle of *échapper*, literally "escaped"— Trans.

that catch one unawares during the slow process of writing. Breaks in the clouds. Visions.

A breakaway from the field by one or several competitors. Breaking away from the field, definitely, but also pulling out of the race. Scramming. Pissing off. Having a nice snooze in the stands.

TRANSLATED FROM THE FRENCH BY WILL HOBSON

EVOLUTION | KAREN CONNELLY

From the Latin verb *evolvere,* to roll out. The common understanding of evolution relates to biology and to Darwin's famous theory—now widely accepted as fact—that all species have developed from earlier forms of life. A more general meaning refers to the gradual development of something—a system, a machine, an idea, an aspect of being—into a more complex and advanced form.

Evolution. Transformation. Transmutation. Change. These are some of our words for being broken, in small and large ways, continually. Form comes to the end of itself, inevitably alters, sprouts newness, a reordering in the mind, the body, the very genes, the molecules, the most basic grit of matter. Philosophy and religion meet biology without argument. They bow to one another and begin to dance. Evolution is the perpetual struggle: of the individual animal; of every species; of human society; of increasingly burdened ecosystems; of this single biosphere.

The evolution of human consciousness is mapped in the history of the novel. A fine novel portrays the evolution of a world, an imaginary ecosystem. Individuals, like the characters in a story, gain consciousness (or do not) by cracking (or not) out of the shell of unknowing, coming to the end of the system, creating a new one. We alter, evolve through decades of experience, stepping more deeply into aliveness (these rich, then richer years) as death rises up to greet us. The irony is so great as to be theatrical, arranged, tragicomic.

Love in the heart, terror in the heart: these are the twin sisters of the novel and of life. Terrifying, and lovely, this evolution of self into spirit, flesh into wisdom, into death, ashes, dust, molecules again, carbon and air.

Finally the wind scatters the heart.

F

FAIRE | CHRISTINE ANGOT

I have chosen *faire* first and foremost because it is a verb, and the verb is God,[1] and because verbs can be conjugated, and that is what writing is: writing is time, is tenses. And because at school they always told us that, wherever possible, we should replace it because, they said, "to do" was ugly and vague, because there was always an alternative to "to do." To do the groceries: to shop; to do the dishes: to wash; to do the laundry: to launder. Instead of saying "to do horseback riding," Marie-Osmonde insisted, we could say "to ride"—indeed, we should say "to ride." She said this with great conviction; she

---

1. A reference to the Gospel according to John (1:1). Where the Revised King James Version reads: "In the beginning was the Word, and the Word was with God, and the Word was God," the French translates the Greek *Logos* as "the Verb": "Au commencement était le Verbe et le Verbe était auprès de Dieu et le Verbe était Dieu."

owned horses—she did not "have" horses. To have, to be, to do, to make—all these verbs presented the same problem. Or, rather, the same difficulty. Rather than "problem," we were told to say "difficulty," "snag," "obstacle," "impediment." To make out: to imply; to do the cooking: to cook; to do housework: to tidy up; to make up: to invent; etcetera. It was always possible. Whenever we saw the verbs "to do" or "to make," we had to hunt them down and eradicate them. If we followed her advice, our compositions would be the richer for it. But: "to make a book."[2] What could be clearer than "to make a book"? To make it. Books should not be written; they should be made.

TRANSLATED FROM THE FRENCH BY FRANK WYNNE

FILLE | ALAIN FLEISCHER

The semantic contours of the word *fille*—that is, girl and/or daughter—are very specific to the French language. This can be seen in the two pairs—or in the trio—that this word forms with the word *fils*, or son, and the word *garçon*, meaning boy. On the one hand, the daughter is the female offspring for which the male equivalent is the son (the youngest daughter can complement the oldest son). On the other hand, the girl is the feminine of the boy. (There were once schools for girls and schools for boys, now regrettably replaced by coeducation.) In the double relation to the son (that is, the

---

2. The phrase "faire un livre" refers both to the writing of a book and the making, printing, and binding of the physical object.

brother) and to the boy (the young individual of the other sex), there is an incestuous dimension of the girl (which we find elsewhere as well, in the ambiguous expression "Daddy's little girl"). The sexual connotation of the word "girl" is taken even further in expressions such as "fille perdue" (lost), "fille de joie" (of joy), "fille publique" (public), "fille du trottoir" (of the sidewalk)—that is, more or less respectively, loose woman, hooker, prostitute, streetwalker. This girl has definitely left her family and is on a path that cuts her off from mother and father, from brothers and sisters. She has become an only child, an orphan girl. When I was a little boy (and a big brother), girls were my sister and all her school friends: there was a girls' side rubbing against my boys' side. Even after all this time, an intimate moment, a shared complicity, a former attraction makes me still call them girls and to see in the crystalline flash of this word the women who surround me as well as those I imagine, which I invent as the female figures in my novels. My middle-aged narrator sees himself more often than not as someone who can't go without the company of girls or of very old men. Adult characters of an intermediary age are absent. However, I don't see this absence as distaste for maturity because it is from this place that I speak, the place where I avoid looking at myself in the mirror. Through speech the old men draw me toward death; through their bodies the girls keep me alive. Together they constitute the texture and the tension of what I write.

TRANSLATED FROM THE FRENCH BY ANN KAISER

FURNITURE | JONATHAN LETHEM

However appalling to consider, however tedious to enact, every novel requires furniture, whether it is to be named or unnamed, for the characters will be unable to remain in standing positions for the duration of the story. For that matter, when night falls—whether it is depicted or occurs between chapters—characters must be permitted to sleep in beds, to rinse their faces in sinks, to glance into mirrors, and so on. (It is widely believed that after Borges, mirrors are forbidden as symbols in novels. However, it is cruel to deny the characters in a novel sight of their own faces; hence mirrors must be provided.) These rules apply no matter how tangential the novel's commitment to so-called realism, no matter how avant-garde or capricious, no matter how revolutionary or bourgeois. Furniture may be explicit or implicit, visible or invisible; may bear the duty of conveying social and economic detail or be merely cursorily functional; may be stolen or purchased, borrowed, destroyed, replaced; may be sprinkled with crumbs of food or splashed with drink; may remain immaculate; may be transformed into artworks by aspiring bohemians; may be inherited by characters from uncles who die before the action of the novel begins; may reward careful inspection of the cushions and seams for loose change that has fallen from pockets; may be collapsible, portable; may even be dragged into the house from the beach where it properly belongs—but, in any event, it must absolutely exist. Anything less is cruelty.

H

HAPPINESS | WEI-WEI

What is happiness? I ask myself the question but don't have a ready-made answer. Yet one thing is sure: I know it. For me happiness is not something abstract or a goal to be attained but rather the accumulation of the countless happy moments that life has kept in store for me and will keep in store for me. The question is to know how to catch them in midair and live them to the fullest.

When I fell in love, I was happy; when I learned I was pregnant, I was happy; when my sons were born, I was happy; when I kissed their little pink cheeks as they came out of school, I was happy; when I bit greedily into the first chocolate cake that they had concocted with their clumsy hands, I was happy; when I came home after a long day of work, I was happy; when I walked into a theater for the first time in my life, I was happy; when I strolled through the small labyrinthine streets of Beijing, Paris, Rome, Cairo, or Edinburgh, I was happy; when

I chatted with several Tibetan women at the edge of a dusty road between Yunnan and Tibet, I was happy; when I walked around the villages of Miao and Tong, nestled in the mountainous folds of Guangxi, I was happy; when I discovered the *tulou* of the Hakka—large dwellings of dried earth circular, square, or rectangular in shape that housed entire clans for ten, twenty, or thirty generations—I was happy; when I share a joke with some friends, I am happy; when I meet a girlfriend whom I haven't seen in a long time, I am happy; when I laugh on the phone with my ninety-five-year-old grandmother, I am happy; when I play a game of mahjong with my husband and children, I am happy; when I come upon a beautiful sentence or a word rich in imagery in my reading, I am happy; when the smell of a delicious dish or the fragrance of a good tea fills my quivering nostrils, I am happy; when I happen to hear a song that reminds me of a delightful moment, I am happy; when I open the window and feel a gentle and refreshing breeze caressing my cheek, I am happy. It is these luminous moments and many others—sometimes very brief but always very real, and as palpable and essential as salt and rice—that warm my heart by softening the hard blows of fate, and make me feel that in spite of EVERYTHING life is worth living.

Happiness is not a destination; it is a path that goes its way. It is not to be looked for beyond the next surmounted obstacles, crossed rivers, conquered mountains, or traversed deserts; we've reached it, it is here, now; and we gather a drop of it every step of the way when we stretch out our hands.

TRANSLATED FROM THE FRENCH BY CATHERINE TEMERSON

In 1989 I witnessed the fall of the Berlin Wall. On that drizzly afternoon I found myself at a spot on Alexanderplatz where ten or so meters of wall had crumbled. Countless Berliners were also there, shouting and jumping for joy. That day I wrote the following note:

> The traditional notion of realism needs to be reformulated and enriched. Life is the product of an accumulation of strata and of traces left by time. Sometimes it cleaves to the course of history, while other times it flows in the form of a dream. I deeply believe that every person's story, along with the place that dreams occupy in the life of every individual, are an essential part of reality. The subjective and the objective must not be separated. The narrator need not cling to the point of view of a character in the first or third person; he should show and compare different points of view. There is nothing to prevent one from rendering a diversity of points of view about the same character or event and weaving all these threads together into a theme. The most objective description never succeeds in faithfully restoring reality. Since realistic writing cannot capture life, one must try to invent a style that comes closer to it: these are my reflections on the form of the novel.

To this note I added: "Try to reflect the reality of the world by reinterpreting traditional narratives." Since then I have written *The Old Garden*, in which I subverted the traditional discourse, and then *The Guest*, *Shim Chong*, *The Odyssey of*

Lotus Flower, and *Princess Bari*. My purpose in writing these novels was to reflect the reality of the world by way of traditional Asian forms. The themes I developed can be summed up in two words: harmony and reconciliation.

I have spent the past four years in London and Paris. It was while staying in London that I had the idea for *Princess Bari*, and it was in Paris that I put the story down on paper. In this modern adaptation of the shaman myth, a North Korean refugee passes through China on his way to London. I took a great interest in some articles in *The Guardian* on the lives of immigrants in London: various religious, ethnic, and cultural communities, made up mainly of former colonial subjects, turned London into a colorful patchwork, like the skin of a panther.

I regard the problem of North Korean refugees as the shadow of globalization. All the world's peripheries suffer from poverty to one degree or another. Even after the cold war, millions of people died in many parts of the world. In North Korea famine and malnutrition killed more than three million people following the collapse of the Soviet bloc.

I would like to imagine the possibility of existing in a sort of plural harmony, which would transcend cultural, religious, ethnic, and economic differences.

Once upon a time the shaman was like the novelist. By telling stories about man's epic suffering and misery, he assumed the role of healer: because he had experienced suffering, he could propose solutions to the human predicament.

TRANSLATED FROM THE KOREAN BY JAY OH

Whenever I think about novels, I think about pleasure. For me the novel is the most complicated—and most enjoyable—experiment with pleasure.

The hedonism of the art of the novel takes three forms: (a) the hedonism of the novelist, (b) the hedonism of the reader, and (c) the hedonism of the character.

The novelist's form of hedonism is motivated by fidelity to the spirit of the nonserious. The seductions of the theological or the political—all the everyday absolutes—are resisted in the name of a more zigzagging dedication to pleasure. Instead of absolute truths, the novelist delights in relativity, in the freedom of absolute accuracy.

As for the reader, his hedonism is an upside-down version of the novelist's. This kind of reading is not intent on information—the everyday certainties. No, the reader as hedonist enjoys a novel's intricate play of form, its thematic inversion of ideas: its infinite horizontal detail.

But, then, there are so many obstacles to pleasure! And pleasure, in the end, is the only concern of any novel's characters—as long as one remembers that pleasure is so difficult to define, so endless in its ingenuity. In the characters of Stendhal, of Kafka, of Hrabal—and other novelists I love—the characters are ingenious at discovering triumph where no one would expect to triumph: in the utter obviousness of their defeat. There can be a pleasure in failure: that is one way of defining what we mean by the comic. Everyone makes do with the freedom they can discover.

And this, I think, is the central aspect of the novel's philosophy of hedonism—for the novelist, and the novel reader, and the novel's characters. Pleasure is unexpected. It will make do with anything.

So in some ways this definition of the novel's hedonism requires another definition: its secret twin. For where else is this omnivorous ingenuity found, where else is real life suspended in this inverted way, if not in the playful seriousness of the erotic?

HERETIC | ANDRÉ BRINK

For me writing has always occurred under the sign of the *heretic*. In *La Croisade albigeoise* Monique Zerder-Chardovoine explains her view of the significance of this concept:

> *Hérésie* vient du mot qui signifie *choix* en grec: pour qu'il y ait hérésie il faut qu'il y ait une idéologie, à laquelle adhère une communauté, ce qu'à l'intérieur de cette communauté des hommes s'en séparent, n'acceptant plus l'ensemble des vérités reçues mais choisissant parmi elles: l'hérésie est une conclusion dont le choix vient de l'entendement humain, en contradiction avec l'écriture sainte et qui est énoncée publiquement et soutenue avec obstination.

> [*Heresy* comes from the word meaning "choice" in Greek: For heresy to exist there must be an ideology to which a community adheres and from which, inside this community, men separate themselves, no longer accepting the entirety of the received truths but choosing among them: heresy is a conclusion whose choice

derives from human understanding, in contradiction to holy writ, and which is publicly stated and obstinately supported.]

For most of my life my writing has been done *against* apartheid, which was the dominant ideology of my country, and its denial of human dignity and values. And behind apartheid as a system stood the notion and the experience of the *abuse of power*, which to me is the primary threat against the freedom of expression without which a writer cannot exist. It goes without saying that writing is not only *against* certain things but also *for* some, like freedom, truth, justice. But in most human societies any celebration of these positive values inevitably sets one on a collision course against the banalities and slogans of the majority, and in this sense a spirit of resistance—even of Camusian *revolt*—must form a major part of the dynamic that lends to writing its passion, its texture, its teleological effectiveness. This leads to the attempts of the majority to exclude or ostracize or oppress the writer as a free spirit: an individual who has chosen, like Antigone, to say *No*—but this is possibly the most positive *No* the world has ever encountered. This kind of heretic finds his or her image in Don Quixote, the knight with the sad countenance who looks past the surfaces and semblances of the world to discover the deeper, stranger, more unsettling truths which lurk behind these, and to do battle with them.

And I hope sincerely to remain faithful to this heresy, this ultimate choice, until the day of my death.

It may seem a strange quality to look for in an art that lives by lies or—to put it more diplomatically—by inventions. But there is such a thing as honesty not of detail but of feeling. Without it no piece of writing is properly alive. Its lies have no depth; they lack the complexity of honesty. The difference between a dishonest text and an honest one is as stark as that between an artificial flower and a real one. It's not a matter of quality but of life.

Authors have to master impersonation, lying, acting; they live as intensely in imaginary worlds as in the real one. But any successful piece of writing must have a seed of honesty or truthfulness beneath all the fiction. It's permissible—even required—that one lie to a reader. But you have to be honest with yourself. Only then will the reader follow. If I claim to be a Norwegian customs woman, or a German stuntman, or a potholer, or a kindergarten teacher, no reader will accuse me of lying. What the reader would find unpardonable would be the failure to make these lies plausible, not to be honest in my dishonesty.

This being honest with yourself is not easy. It means living without illusions and—almost inevitably—without belief (and not just in God). It means exposing yourself to cynicism without becoming cynical (because cynicism, like any other denial of self, is a form of lie).

TRANSLATED FROM THE GERMAN BY MICHAEL HOFMANN

I

"I" | RACHID EL-DAÏF

"I": a lever. A worker's tool.

With a simple lever and a few other tools one can build pyramids as immense as the pyramids of Egypt. One can construct terraces on the rockiest and most isolated mountains. One can transport the heaviest stones to uninhabited regions. I have had the personal experience of building a house in an isolated corner of the Lebanese mountains. During that experience, the lever was the most useful tool of all, without which the problems I was confronted with would have been impossible to solve.

Likewise the "I" in certain cases is like a lever, a mighty instrument which is, above all, quite adequate.

For example, the "I" allows me personally to place myself inside the skin of some other character I would not want to be, allows me to adopt his logic and see with his eyes.

And it allows me to write a novel that gives the impression of having taken place in my own past, as if it were the most personal and intimate account of my own life. The reader thus acquires two pleasures: that of reading a novel and that of spying through the keyhole and seeing what is going on behind closed doors. Like many other people, I think that the novel as a genre is based upon that particular human curiosity called voyeurism.

I like writing in the first person. It makes me feel completely at ease; with it I can enjoy almost total freedom.

"I" is a lever.

TRANSLATED FROM THE FRENCH BY PAULA HAYDAR

IDENTITIES | NURUDDIN FARAH

I was in trouble with my teacher on my first day at school. The school was a multi-stream community school, which my father had a hand in establishing in the small farming town of Kallafo, in the Somali-speaking, Ethiopia-administered Ogaden. I was the fourth son of a large family, five years old, a little mischievous, restless, and I did not get on well with my father, who was authoritarian and could not abide my frequent back talk.

On that day I had gone to school with my eldest brother, who helped carry the chair I was to sit on, given that I was too short. My eldest brother left me in the care of the brother whom I came after. He told me to behave; otherwise the teacher would cane me. When our teacher, whom I knew—

because he and his family lived in our compound, in houses belonging to my father—arrived, all the pupils except me got up and did not sit down until he said, "Now sit down, class."

His eyes falling sharply on me, he instructed me to rise to my feet. When I did so, he said, "Who are you? And what is your name?" As I knew that he knew me, that he had in fact sent me to get his wife some sugar earlier that morning, I responded that I did not know who I was, and that I had forgotten my name. My teacher caned me for what he considered back talk. I received further punishment when I met my father.

Later, as an adult and a writer, I got into political trouble with Somalia's dictator, whose security, I believed, was intent on harming me physically. Afraid, paranoid, I would travel under guises to places I considered dangerous, on occasion giving myself other identities and claiming to be someone else. However, I remember an embarrassing moment in New York, in 1989, when I called on Chinua Achebe at an NYU-run apartment block in which he was staying. A Somali on duty at the reception desk approached and asked if I was "Nuruddin Farah." I said I was not. Appalled, Achebe turned to me and said, "But you are. Why do you not admit who you are?"

Maybe all my life I have been trying to unravel the strands of my known and unknown identities and writing about their many strains, if only to make sure that I have a multiple selfhood too cumbersome to unscramble. Perhaps there lie the defining characteristics of a novelist?

Venice, November, cold, gray, and foggy. I'm walking through Piazza San Marco to the café at the Campanile. The window panes of the café are misted. Suddenly a woman's hand inside starts rubbing the panes clean. In Alfred Andersch's novel *Die Rote*, there is such a scene. The sudden memory moves me deeply with an enormous force. Reading this book immediately is more important than anything else. I take the night train home, stop at a bookstore, and read the novel in one sitting, shrouded in the fatigue of the night trip and the feverish curiosity of memory. As I read, an idea I never thought was in me takes shape nearly imperceptibly: Why get drawn into the vortex of a story only by reading? Why not write a story myself? That was the prelude to my first novel. I soon felt the fever of imagination; it was like a wonderful search, and I have never recovered from it. At first I seemed to be bound only by the story and its logic. Later I grasped it was something else that was much more important than the story: the insights into myself expressed in it. Our imagination, fed by the sources of the unconscious, is very wise. Its meandering ways show us who we really are, beyond all social roles. That is, our life isn't what we live on the outside but rather what we imagine we live.

TRANSLATED FROM THE GERMAN BY BARBARA HARSHAV

INDIA | TARUN J. TEJPAL

An arrow through time, whispering like a flute.

A single arching tree out of varying roots.

The secure-safe home with no trace of a roof.

The elephant's tread, implacable and mild.

A fearful symmetry, the Bengal tiger in the wild.

The cobra's flaring hood; the rhino's rare hide.

The dance of Shiva, ascetic and king.

The grace of Devi beyond all asking.

Balm of the Buddha; the lacerations of caste;

Bloody daggers of religion drawn from the past.

Dazzle of machines.

Money's magnetic shine.

In the hearts of technology,

The deity's antique shrine.

Lessons of the Mahabharata:

The puzzle of life.

Broad shoulders of brotherhood.

Feudalism's sharp knife.

Dharma, the duty. Kama, the desire.

Freedom by moksha. Rebirth by fire.

A hundred tongues. A billion throats.

Pain-pleasure's philosophy in every note.

The music of cruelty under nonviolence's veneer.

The song of greed in the land of the fakir.

Sweet shade of ficus; the holy Ganga's flow.

Beloved of the gods; eternity's favorite whore.

A little less of India; of India a little more.

INSOMNIA | LUDMILA ULITSKAYA

Of all the varieties of exasperating, tormenting insomnia,

I am going to write about just one, which, for want of a better word, I shall call creative insomnia. When I was young I even devoted a poem to it, of which I can now recall only one stanza:

I love the distance of insomnias,
The luminescence of their far horizons,
The secret meanings behind their mists,
Though sleep be even further out of reach.

Waking at night and falling asleep again most resembles an illness in childhood when all sense of reality is lost with the onset of fever, and the boundary between dream and reality becomes blurred, and you break through from the solidity of the everyday world into the yielding realms of fantasy. Insomnia is the most natural conduit to Plato's world of the ideal, to Alice's Wonderland, to the tripod of the Oracle, to purgatory and hell and, indeed, to the creative laboratory of the good Lord himself. It is a spontaneous breakthrough, unlike the conscious and deliberate breakthrough in pursuit of which in every age millions have resorted to alcohol, drugs, and practices unfamiliar to ordinary people. It is the kind of breakthrough sometimes made in the throes of passion and creative ecstasy.

In the 1920s Osip Mandelshtam, a great Russian poet, in a radio broadcast on the subject of the young Goethe spoke of the "cavalry of insomnias" that spurred his creativity. Insomnia is linked to man's creative faculty and nurtures it, but sleep deprivation is also a torment, as present-day torturers well know.

The insomnia I am talking about results from a mild state of possession, harmless to those around you, who sometimes even fail to notice it. It usually comes when you are completely engrossed in your work and overtakes you so completely that every aspect of your daily life becomes mechanical and provides only a colorless backdrop to action occurring only in your mind.

It matters not whether at this time you are asleep or awake. The secret life pulses within you, and when you wake in the middle of the night you realize there is no way to stem its flow. The stillness of the sleeping house, sleeping children, sleeping things is so entrancingly transparent that, very, very quietly, you get out of bed, set the kettle to boil, and—with a cup of tea and a pencil, in a state close to weightlessness, almost sleepwalking—scribble something incredibly important in your notebook, abbreviating words, leaving out letters. Waking in the morning, you sometimes cannot even understand what felicitous snippets came to mind, what those important thoughts were which have vanished without a trace, what words, sluiced and purified, have fluttered away, never to return. At least not before your next sleepless night.

Actually there have been many instances of great discoveries made by scientists while they slept. Mendeleev claimed that his brilliant periodic table of the chemical elements came to him in a dream. Vladimir Mayakovsky told of how he had been pursuing an image for three days when the word needed for a poem also came to him in a dream. In the middle of the night, he wrote down on a cigarette packet "sole remaining leg," only to puzzle over the meaning of these odd words in the morning. Thus, a famous poem was born:

> I fear to forget your name, as a poet fears to forget
> some word born laboriously in the night,
> its magnitude equivalent to god.
> I shall tend and love your body
> as a soldier amputated by war, unneeded, unwanted,
> loves his sole remaining leg.

Blessed is insomnia. Especially for the chosen few who do not have to leap out of bed when the alarm goes off, to descend to the underworld of the metro with a briefcase in their hand and breakfast in their pocket, to drag a cranky child to school and then get on for the next eight hours with doing their desk job, their work, their stint.

TRANSLATED FROM THE RUSSIAN BY ARCH TAIT

ISLAND | ERRI DE LUCA

For those who belong to the Mediterranean, "island" was a means of escape, a fortuitous landing, a hideout, unleashed dogs, blinding limestone. Only later would it be reduced to a vacation spot.

The powers that be misunderstood "island." For them it was an enclosure to be perfected with bars. The powers that be built prison cells on the islands, sending their opponents there to rot. The next to the last to do so were the monarchy and fascism; the last was the republic: the same fantasy of cramming prisoners into the infamous prisons of Asinara, Favignana, Procida, Elba, Pianosa. Even in France, where islands are few and far between, a rock facing Marseille served the purpose.

"Island" instead is the wide-open horizon, big enough to embrace any of its terraces. "Island" is always on the leeward side. It is the occupation of the seas, pirates, watchtowers, castaways and shipwrecks, rainwater barrels. Islands are thirsty. People who stay gain in faith; those who leave gain in betrayal, the first step of every fortune.

For me "island" was learning to place bait on hooks, wash my wounds in seawater, sit silently in a boat, get sunburned—even for the sake of love—without seeking shade. Island is a teacher. Those who do not love one are destined to get lost in the dark without a candle.

"Island" is a shell, the sea rising into a tempest is the muscle that closes and seals it. "Island" is swimming in the high seas and discovering that fishermen don't know how to swim. In their eyes I learned the shame of having a superfluous skill. You can tell an island from the mainland.

Today it is an enclosure for emigrants, trapped between guards and bars, guilty of travel, after crossing latitudes. Today Lampedusa is our calling card: tourism and prison.

TRANSLATED FROM THE ITALIAN BY MICHAEL F. MOORE

L

TO LAST | GIUSEPPE CULICCHIA

"Il faut d'abord durer"—first, one must last—as Ernest Hemingway liked to say.[1] Whatever opinion we may have about the author of *Fiesta*, aka *The Sun Also Rises*, whether we love or hate the man based on our personal tastes—or what we think our personal tastes should be subject to our education, what we read, and the company we keep—it seems to me this statement of his regarding the writer's craft is very important, very true—though it can also be very painful and, moreover, always relevant. The only thing that really counts for a writer or his work—beyond what his critical

----

1. Ernest Hemingway had a favorite expression: "il faut d'abord durer." He used the saying in his private letters and on occasion inscribed the words in books he signed for friends. The French saying translates as "first, one must last." Hemingway is a writer who truly has lasted. He has earned the distinction of being called timeless—trans.

success or favor with the public might be; regardless of literary awards he may or may not receive or the number of times he appears on so-called cultural television shows—is that he manage to last over time. That his works still be read ten or a hundred years after publication. That they continue to stir people's emotions through changing times and succeeding generations. Only by doing so can a writer truly consider himself a writer, it seems to me, whether or not he has received a Nobel Prize in literature. The problem is that, except in very rare cases, the average life of a writer usually does not allow him to ascertain whether his works—or at least one of them—are destined to last. Another Ernest, or, rather, Ernst, Herr Jünger, perhaps had the opportunity to do so: dying at 102 years of age and therefore able to know that his books were reprinted over the decades, continually finding new readers, he must have been aware of being truly a writer during his lifetime and beyond. The others, however, have no way of knowing. Unless they have a very high opinion of themselves—and I must say that I reluctantly know some of these—everyone else should in theory depart with some doubt. Assuming the matter is of genuine concern to them, of course.

TRANSLATED FROM THE ITALIAN BY ANNE MILANO APPEL

LAUGHTER | TARIQ ALI

Why do we laugh? How do we laugh? The answers depends on different aspects of our makeup: language, culture, tradition, etcetera. Can there be a truly universal humor? I am skeptical, though the market tries hard to confect a global amusement. U.S. television networks make up for the deficiencies of other nationalities and cultures by introducing canned laughter in comedy shows. There is no longer any need to laugh. It has been sorted out by the producer/director and, like one of Pavlov's dogs, all that is required is for a viewer to sit back and join the fun.

Even jokes about sex and sexuality, which could aspire to universality, are not always appreciated to the same extent, if at all, by every culture. Take a traditional popular anecdote from South Asia: "A nobleman fucking his wife's maidservant could not manage an erection. He instructed her to take his penis in her mouth and help him. As she did so, he farted. The maidservant began to laugh and the limp penis dropped out. He said: 'What is there to laugh about? I'm not Suleyman [Solomon] that I can command the wind.' 'No', she replied, 'and I'm not Isa [Jesus] that I can bring the dead back to life.'" This might bring a smile to the face of a Westerner, who understand the references, but would a Confucian appreciate it at all?

The way we laugh is equally related to class and culture. For instance, formerly in most cultures refined women were taught that laughter was vulgar and that, if they were tempted to do so, their hand should cover their mouth. There is a Punjabi saying: "Hansi te phansi" (She laughs, she's yours). Even in the case of men, loud laughter was generally regarded as the privilege of peasants and the "lower orders," except for gentleman who had drunk too much and could be forgiven. In some ways these traditions persist. Unaffected laughter remains a subversive act.

LIES | ADRIAAN VAN DIS

No better source for stories than malleable memory. The older you get, the faster you used to run when you were young. The longer ago the war, the more people were in the Resistance. Even the battered wife kids herself that she loves her man. Lies provide consolation. Listen to those lies, write them down, and from that labyrinth of contradictory memories let a new lie come forth—one that may actually come close to the truth. The most intractable lies are the National Lies. They, too, are a good source of material for the writer. The Dutch, for instance, have deluded themselves into thinking they are a hospitable people. It is said that we welcome the stranger with open arms. As a people we know not of xenophobia. This splendid concept was easy to sustain as long as the number of foreigners remained modest, but now that my country finds itself overrun with immigrants, our vaunted hospitality has revealed itself to be but a thin veneer. As a writer, it is satisfying to scratch at that veneer. To summon up characters who hold up a mirror to ourselves.

One of our most intractable national lies is our Dutch cleanliness. We have persuaded ourselves that we are a nation of sidewalk scrubbers, window washers, and rug beaters. Our country is supposed to be an immaculately raked park:

hemmed in by dikes, carved into tidy rectangular parcels, trimmed, pruned, rinsed clean by tamed rivers, canals, and ditches. A self-cleaning water-state where nature doesn't dare to make a mess.

No wonder Baudelaire—who was dirt-phobic (known for his pronouncement "Many friends means many gloves") and preferred perfume to the smell of fresh flowers—lauds Holland no less than four times for being an immaculate man-made paradise: "Là, tout n'est qu'ordre et beauté [...] Où tout est riche, propre et luisant."[2] Not that the poet ever visited our polders, the land reclaimed from the sea; he never got any farther than Antwerp, and for poetry's sake that's probably just as well, for the truth would surely have spoiled his dream. Only in the imagination could he hope to find such a spotless paradise.

Where does the notion of all those clean Dutch people come from? From the domestic scenes of the Golden Age, those paintings redolent of green soap? Maidservants busy with their pots and pans, housewives sweeping, mothers fussing over their brood, and all those gleaming interiors showing cupboards brimming with linens (e.g., by Pieter de Hooch or Pieter van den Bosch or Gerard ter Borch). . . . Yes, even in Jan Steen's *The Disorderly Household* a person could eat off the floor. That, apparently, was how the Dutch liked to see themselves: clean as a whistle.

---

2. "There, where there is nothing but order and beauty . . . Where everything is rich, clean, and sparkling."

The glorification of the broom, however, touches not so much on physical cleanliness as on the need for moral purity. ("Wash the hands, ye sinners, and purify the hearts," wrote Jan Luyken.) It is filthy lucre and the stain of worldly pleasures clinging to it that the seventeenth-century Dutchman wants to wash off. In all those pretty pictures and rhymes about personal cleanliness, it was one's piety, first and foremost, that was being buffed up. Religious devotion professed by soap and broom; a clean stoop the threshold to heaven.

Many couldn't help being taken in. In *The Embarrassment of Riches* the historian Simon Schama cites a slew of foreign visitors to the Low Countries in the Golden Age. All can't say enough about the immaculate Dutch cities and streets: "As clean as any chamber floor." And that image was so persistent, it seems, that it spread far and wide beyond our borders. Pictures of Dutch milkmaids adorn the soaps and polishes of other nations to this day. In the United States Old Dutch Cleanser is a household word.

While the front stoops of the decent burghers were certainly scrubbed spotless, some visitors also ventured around the back. In *The Travellers' Dictionary of Quotations* we find one jeering reference after another to filthy streets, slovenly inns, and a "very dirty and wicked" Amsterdam indeed.

Some visitors paid attention to their noses. Thus we find in many a contemporary journal or letter passages detailing the body odor of those black-clad merchants and churchgoers. "Everything gleams in Holland, within, front door and stoop, but the dirty collars most of all," one anonymous Brit wrote to his wife. One stranger even wondered if the fishermen of the Zuyder Zee might be hiding a fish's tail under their baggy duffel trousers, which reeked of fish and which they never took off. Overseas, too, the Dutchman's personal hygiene was a matter of note. There's a well-known Japanese print of Dutch peddlers in Dejima being pursued by a swarm of flies. In the oral and written literature of black South Africa, the most salient feature of the first Hollanders on the Cape is their sickly-sweet smell.

It must have been the Dutch, then, who designated themselves clean people, just as they fooled themselves into thinking of themselves as tolerant and hospitable. (Although it finally does seem to be sinking in that the latter two qualities are based on a heavy dose of pure indifference.)

Let's take another look in from the outside. Ask the strangers who made our country their home over the past years. The ones repatriated from the former Dutch East Indies, the family environment in which I spent the first decade of my life. People from tropical climes, in the habit of taking a bath every day—even in their new homeland. Every day? Wasn't that a bit much for people dependent on social welfare? And who was supposed to pay for all that hot water?

In the mid-1950s the council sent a social worker round to convince us to mend our profligate ways: bathing once a week ought to be enough. In our house that visit was for a long time recalled with glee. What a joke—those filthy Dutch!

At that time showers were for the first time being installed in rental housing—the wash room as the democratic society's crowning achievement. And what did the people do with their shower? They filled it with junk or used it as a coal cellar. But showering? Dipping your big toe in the tub once a week was more than enough, surely.

We remember hearing stories about the first nurses from Suriname—toward the end of the 1950s—who were so taken aback by the lack of genital hygiene in our country: women who never washed their vaginas; men with a cheesy white ring under their foreskins. People from the tropics were used to giving their private parts a good cleaning. The Dutch considered such a thing indecent.

To this day the Dutchman doesn't smell any sweeter. Since I often find myself out of the country, it strikes me every time I come home.

Stick your nose into one of the rush-hour commuter trains to or from The Hague and check out all those career-frustrated Masters of Arts or Sciences—it's not just the sour stench of their ambitions that will make you gag. Could it be that since the emancipation of the Dutch woman, the Dutchman has grown even more grungy? Consider, too, that over the past twenty years the number of dry cleaners has dwindled by half.

What is it that I mean to say with all this? It is that I, a writer with the nose of a stranger, wish to give my homeland the smell test. So that we don't keep on tooting our own horn. Self-regard stinks.

TRANSLATED FROM THE DUTCH BY HESTER VELMANS

Loyalty is the most important virtue espoused by dynasties of the East. When babies first babbled, they were already taught that the most sacred duty in life was to be "loyal to the King."

In my youth the concept "loyalty to the King" was transformed into "loyalty to the Communist Party." Naturally this concept, as an integral part of "tradition," was readily accepted. Since it only meant the transference of loyalty from the King to the Party, how could that be troublesome?

At twenty I joined the war against the Americans. Reality opened up countless dark pages, causing me to turn the words over. I then realized that they were only cadavers that were not preserved in formaldehyde and therefore smelled like dead toads. That was when I decided to embark on the path of a rebel fighter.

In 1991 the Minister of the Interior came to see me in jail. He said, "How dare you oppose the Party!" I replied, "According to your definition, what is the Party?" Finding him shocked and at a loss for words, I continued: "I look at your Party like this: Over two million Party members obey a Central Committee of three hundred. Then these three hundred obey the Politburo of thirteen individuals. If this number only means thirteen skulls having bean dregs for brains and thirteen depraved characters, then there is no reason whatsoever to be loyal to the Party. The Party is not God up there. The Party is this number thirteen, and, honestly, I only see thirteen pig heads and thirteen scoundrels. Upholding loyalty is no longer my duty."

After that I officially became "the people's enemy" because the regime understood that I had not only deviated from the Party's path but had struck out in the opposite direction. In the struggle against an enemy a million times stronger than I am, my only weapon is scorn, absolute scorn for the rulers.

It has taken me thirty years of fighting as a rebel to master just this one word. What an arduous road! Thanks to that experience, I have come to understand that writing is a job for those who are insane and committed to forced labor, since before using words—the raw material of their works—they have to wrestle with their ghosts in a long-drawn-out, lonely, and fierce contest.

Having said that, I wish all writers—the insane dreamers given to forced labor—ultimate victory!

TRANSLATED FROM THE VIETNAMESE BY BAC HOAI TRAN

M

Language, an ever-evolving process, varies from culture to culture and place to place. In Spanish the word *mariquita* can mean many different things, depending on the country or region. In most of South America a *mariquita* is a ladybug; in the Caribbean it's a saltwater fish; and in Argentina it's a folk dance. Puerto Ricans use the term to identify a rare black-bird with yellow wings, and Costa Ricans give that name to a tree that's indigenous to their country. In Colombia Mariquita is a town in the department of Tolima, near where I grew up. However, without exception in the entire Spanish-speaking world *mariquita* is an offensive, derogatory term for "homosexual."

As a writer, my biggest concern is tolerance. I grew up in a country with a long history of bigotry and fanaticism, which has translated into decades of civil war, marginalization of native Indians and the peasantry, discrimination against women, repression of gays and lesbians, and violations of all sorts of human rights.

When I first set out to write "The Other Widow," a short love story set in rural Colombia, I needed a name for the village where it would take place. As many other stories do, "The Other Widow" deals with the uncharted, mysterious ways of the human heart—except that the two lovers in it just happen to be boys. So I decided that, as a paradox, the prejudiced village where the story would take place would be called Mariquita, literally "little faggot." "The Other Widow" turned out to be the seed of my first novel, *Tales from the Town of Widows*, and Mariquita soon became synonymous with isolation and chaos, a town of widows where all but three men had been press-ganged into fighting in the civil war by guerrilla groups. For sixteen years this group of ordinary women is caught up in a struggle to survive; to overcome their grief, fear, ignorance, and passivity and build a new society of their own on the patriarchal rubble of the old. Ultimately they create a new way of life based on a female perspective of what is right and good: peace, equality, and respect for each individual within the larger, all-important community.

Mariquita, the village, proves to be a vivid setting in which human nature is revealed and culture reinvented. Mariquita, the word, becomes synonymous with freedom, harmony, compromise and progress. Language has continued its ever-evolving process. This time, however, all the meanings are positive and, most important, universal.

"Unfurling" is to me the very action of writing and reading. To be unfurling a story as though unfurling a length of satin cloth from a roll, seeing the spill and run of silk spread out and along, there and there and there. . . . The length of cloth like a slip of river, like a sea. . . . That is writing; that is reading. A sense of abandon, richness, a running on, running into. . . . The text spinning into beautiful lengths and expanses and all of this as though uncontrolled, as though inevitable . . .

And this bolt of satin. . . . It sits restrained and tidy on the shelves amongst the other fabrics. It doesn't show its patina and weave, its extravagant surface and color. . . . It is contained, waiting, in the fabric halls of an old-fashioned department store, I think, the kind of store with wood-and-gilt-trimmed windows, with flat, soft carpets. . . . The kind of store that has large mahogany measuring tables to take the measure of the cloth, the darkness of the wood all the better to unfurl the length along . . .

Waiting for the moment of its unfurling.

Unfurling stories . . .

Unfurling words.

THE STROLLING MIRROR | RODRIGO FRESÁN

One of my favorite definitions of the art of the novel is Stendhal's phrase: "Un roman est un miroir qui se promène le long de la route" [A novel is a mirror that strolls along the road].

And a guilty confession: the first time I encountered it was not in the voice of Stendhal but in Michael Ondaatje's novel *The English Patient*.

As a result of which, for quite a while—even, to my embarrassment, in writing—I attributed the quote to the author born in Ceylon (present-day Sri Lanka) and not to the author born in Grenoble (still in France).

I'll say in my defense that the confusion or misattribution is forgivable, and even justified, because it gives me the justification to state here that the novel is an entity in constant motion, elusive, its DNA always in flux. I don't think there can be two more different and even opposed writers than Stendhal and Ondaatje: the love of unadorned clarity and the cleanly structured plots of the former contrasted with the poetic images and the sudden, disjointed shifts in time and setting of the latter seem two irreconcilable systems that nonetheless meet on the same path in order to watch a mirror go by.

What are they seeking there? What concerns and consumes them? My reading of both writers leads me to think that the questions that concern them are quite different, irreconcilable yet complementary.

It's easy enough to guess that what consumed Stendhal was where that road begins and where Julien Sorel or Fabrizio del Dongo will end up. Ondaatje, on the other hand, will always pause to listen to the different voices that rise up to the rafters of an Italian bell tower or that echo under the arches of a Canadian viaduct.

Then, too, it's possible that both writers are curious to learn who is carrying that mirror, which I never imagine as pocket-sized but instead envision as panoramic and cinemascopic: a mirror as big as the landscape through which it is borne, not by one or two people but by a throng of happy masters enslaved by the honor and privilege of such a burden.

Personally, as a novelist what I most like to tell—or try to make a story out of—is how one person or many people could have come up with the idea of taking a mirror out for a stroll.

Although the notion may have been devised by none other than that mercurial, self-sufficient glass that only reflects what it wants us to see.

In any case, here it comes again, the strolling mirror, on the road.

Look into it; see yourselves.

TRANSLATED FROM THE SPANISH BY NATASHA WIMMER

N

NO | OLIVIA ROSENTHAL

They asked me to choose a word; they explained that each writer was going to choose a word and that they would put together a new dictionary with all the words, which would be a dictionary of chosen words; so you have to choose a word, they said, the hidden word that compelled you to write your last book, the word that generated it, the word at the heart of it without necessarily being visible, the invisible word; you must reveal it, and I said,

No.

That was coolly received. It's always like that. It's chilly. It creates distance. It's not really meant to, but it does. Mostly it's that I can't do anything else. In the beginning I always start off that way. It's not a principle, it's not a posture, it's a completely irrational gesture that catches me off guard every time, because every time I repeat it without thinking about it. I say,

No.

A two-letter word, a little nothing word, a childish word— quick, ridiculous, almost definitive. It's *No*. No, no, and no. No three times.

Later on perhaps we can discuss it; they may convince me I've made a mistake, that I could've said something else, done something else, but in the beginning and above all, as protection, as defense, as resistance, or, more precisely, by default,

No.

Besides, to be totally honest, the distance it creates doesn't bother me—on the contrary. Because in distance one can find access, one can gradually get closer to and learn to tame the other. But when there is no distance, then it gets dangerous, much too dangerous for me.

Can you explain to us why you decided to write about Alzheimer's?

No.

Are the events you talk about in this book ones you've experienced?

No.

And, contrary to what you may think, this is a positive no, a joyous no, a no full of energy; it's the no of someone who has no intention of letting herself be felled. No. To delay the end a bit, to act as if you could, to accord yourself the power to resist, by virtue of a single word.

To explain my position, here's a little anecdote. One day I walk into a bookstore—I'm a devoted reader of Thomas Bernhard; he's a writer I admire a lot—and there, by chance, I come across a book of his that I haven't heard of and whose title strikes me as very unexpected. I say to myself, "That's a beautiful title. Thomas Bernhard has written a book with a very beautiful title. One day I'd like to write a book with that title and, what's more, being familiar with the author, it's surprising, a true revolution in the writing of the master." I buy the book. It's called *Yes*. I go back home, I open it, I read it in one sitting; it's a book one reads in one sitting, breathlessly. It's about a series of conversations between the narrator and a woman called the Persian woman. They take walks together, and during these walks they talk about the forest, music, Schopenhauer, the comparative merits of Switzerland and Austria—in short, it's a Thomas Bernhard book. Finally the Persian woman, who nevertheless has no desire to live in this remote corner of Austria, finds herself there alone because her companion, the Swiss man, goes back to Switzerland and does not return. The walks and conversations continue until the Persian woman disappears. As I read, I search for the meaning of the title; there has not been an upheaval in Thomas Bernhard's writing; this text is just as dark as the others; I don't understand the choice of title; I continue to read; I'm more and more intrigued by a Yes that does not resonate with what I am reading. I think to myself, "Maybe this is a book of suspense. Thomas Bernhard has written a book of suspense; you have to wait for the end; you have to wait for the final word, for the last word of the book, for the riddle finally to be solved." And here is the end: "Quite out of the blue and, in fact, in my tactless way I had asked the Persian woman if she would kill herself one day. Upon which she had only laughed and said *Yes*." I put down Thomas Bernhard's book, I cried, and I laughed. I laughed for thinking that Thomas Bernhard or one of his characters would for once emerge from rage and despair. I laughed at the trick he played on me. I laughed at my mistake. And right afterward I thought the Persian woman may have said yes but I say no.

No?

No.

TRANSLATED FROM THE FRENCH BY JEANINE HERMAN

NO WHY | YANNICK HAENEL

Twice in Western history we have heard the resounding "no why." Thus, Angelus Silesius, in the midst of the Middle Ages, described the palpitation of the poetical: "The rose has no why" [Die rose ist ohne warum], he wrote. No causality determines the blooming of the rose; it exists for nothing—and this disinterestedness coincides with what we call poetry.

The second time it was Primo Levi who referred to "no why." It was in a concentration camp in Auschwitz. Primo Levi was thirsty. A snowdrift had formed against a window. He went out of the barracks, wanting to break off a piece of ice to quench his thirst. A German Kapo stops him: "Why?" asks Primo Levi. "Hier ist kein warum" (Here there is no why) answers the Nazi.

The "no why" in this case is the very opposite of Angelus Silesius's experience—the precise opposite of poetic disinterestedness: the watchword of a devastated world; the very sign of barbarity; the fundamental absurdity of that world.

What existence there is today is felt through the twofold experience of "no why."

For this twofold experience—the constant possibility that poetry may appear and the virtual summons of each body to destruction—comes up against the empty core of representation, that is to say, the unrepresentable.

To write in the twenty-first century is to become the witness to the unrepresentable. It is to make audible, through words, both contemporary abjection (the forbidden snowdrift) and the possibility of delight (the rose). It is to tap into what currently exists of the vein of evil and poetic openness.

TRANSLATED FROM THE FRENCH BY DEBORAH FURE

NOMAD | ELIF SHAFAK

There is a metaphor that is close to my heart. The holy book of Islam mentions an unusual tree called the tuba. Sometimes this heavenly tree is said to be upside down. It has its roots up in the air instead of having them in the ground. Sometimes I think writing fiction resembles spreading out your branches like the tuba tree. It is true that human beings thrive and survive through and upon their roots. But, unlike trees, human beings can have peripatetic roots—or portable homelands. Similarly, fiction writing has deep roots, but these are not necessarily grounded in one particular territory or one fixed identity. As a writer, my roots are up in the air. In this way I feel connected to many places and cities at once. My fiction is both local and universal. It is both deeply Turkish and cosmopolitan. My writing strives to transcend national and religious and gender and class boundaries.

Ever since I was a child, life has been a nomadic journey. First physically, then intellectually and spiritually. A nomad is not an immigrant. These two are different ways of being. The twentieth century has seen an influx of immigrants moving once and for all from one corner of the world to Western cities miles and cultures away. But an immigrant is not someone who would like to make that move an incessant project. Rather, he would like to settle down in new territory. As such, the immigrant is usually future-oriented and clearly distinguishes between the past and the present, the country he has left behind and the one he now belongs to. The nomad lives in a "perpetual present moment." To live the life of a nomad means to be able to make new friendships, meet new challenges, but most of all to let go—of your possessions, of your old self. A sorrowful enrichment attends the soul in the course of this quest. A nomad or commuter is always wandering, if not physically then spiritually. Wherever he goes he carries within himself an undying sense of estrangement. Paradoxically, he is equally "at home" in different places.

There is a nomad in my novels. My writing thrives upon journeys between cultures and an endless quest. I believe it is possible to have multiple roots—to be both a modern, secular novelist following the great Western traditions of literature and, at the same time, to be inspired by religious philosophy, cultural history, Eastern traditions, local customs, folk Islam, and particularly Sufism.

THE NOVEL AS WEB | A. S. BYATT

My word for the *The Novelist's Lexicon* is "Web." This word in English connotes both a tapestry woven on a loom and the webs woven by spiders to catch their prey. The art of the novel is to construct a fabric that can contain and connect almost an infinity of observations, concepts, human beings, societies, languages, colors, and places in almost an infinity of patterns. The novel is a metaphor for the world, and the knots, or crossing-places within the web of the novel, are its internal metaphors. Michel Butor, in his fine essay "Le Roman comme recherche" [The Novel as Research] writes: "J'appelle 'symbolisme' d'un roman l'ensemble des relations de ce qu'il nous décrit avec la réalité où nous vivons. . . ." [I call "symbolism" of a novel the totality of relations of what it describes to us with the reality within which we live]. He continues: "Le symbolisme externe du roman tend à se réfléchir dans un symbolisme interne. . . ." [The external symbolism of the novel tends to be reflected by an internal symbolism.]

As a student I worked on the levels of allegory in Dante's *Divina Commedia*—the literal, the allegorical, the moral, and the anagogical—and I learned to be passionately excited by words and events that had different meanings within different patterns in the same text. It follows that the novelists I love are those who make interwoven patterns. I love Proust, whose world is both a social comedy, an essay on aesthetics, a history, and a bravura pattern of endlessly changing metaphors, from cathedrals to hawthorn. I love Balzac's *Human Comedy,* which is both a scientific treatise, a dense social history, a vision of good and evil, and a human drama. I love Herman Melville, whose marine metaphors contain a biology, a spiritual vision, a microcosm of America, an ocean, and a narrative of a voyage. I love Henry James, who himself loved webs and wrote of art and life as a *Figure in the Carpet.* I love Thomas Mann, who made a microcosm of a clinic with Wagnerian symbolism, and a tale of Faust that was a study of modern music and an analysis of the tragic disintegration of Hitler's Germany. And in England I love George Eliot, whose *Middlemarch* is an ordinary English town and a spiritual place—"Nel mezzo del cammin di nostra vita." She, too, has strands of science and strands of religion—and strands of fairy tale and strands of rural comedy—in her complicated, singular web. As Butor implies, these symbolic forms also resemble the repeated, self-containing Mandelbrot sets in the geometry of chaos. The novel is as precise, as chaotic, and as various in its forms as Melville's ocean.

NOVEL/LIFE | JAMES MEEK

Novel, masculine noun: a form of literature prevalent in Europe and the Americas which once pretended to imitate life but has since acquired a shallow, unrealistic form unrelated to the actual world of existence.

Life, feminine noun: a form of existence prevalent in Europe and the Americas which once pretended to imitate the novel but has since acquired a shallow, unrealistic form unrelated to the actual world of literature.

WHAT IS THE NOVEL? | ALAA EL ASWANY

I like the definition of the novel as: "Life on paper, resembling our daily life, except that it has more depth, meaning, and beauty."

What I try to accomplish while writing is not ideas or issues; rather, it is characters, living characters, carrying the ideas and propelling the drama forward until they meet their destiny in the end, exactly as happens in our real life. I work for months on end on the characters, carefully noting the details of each one of them as if making a doll. I try to capture the minutest details. If that character is a man: How old is he? How much does he weigh? What kind of clothes does he wear? Does he smoke and even what kind of cigarettes does he smoke? I keep adding these details until the moment arrives when I can see these characters with astonishing clarity. When that moment occurs I know they are no longer imagined characters but rather here, with me, in the room. At that point, just as you might accompany a group of friends on an outing, I accompany the characters on the journey that is the novel.

When I have them all well in mind, I begin writing. At that stage I have only a general, broad idea about how the action will unfold, and that will usually change as events proceed. Writing then takes care of itself, correcting itself as it proceeds. The biggest surprise, however, comes a little later, after a few chapters: at some wonderful moment that words cannot describe, the characters come alive in a real way; they acquire a will independent of mine, in such a way that it becomes impossible for me to impose on them anything they don't want. It is then that I change from an author to an observer. Every morning I record what I see on the screen of my imagination. The happiness that comes over me as I relate what my characters do very much resembles what a father feels when he attends his children's weddings or graduations: they've grown up and are now independent. You have to step aside so that they can live their lives, away from your intervention.

This feeling of happiness in this case is not pure; rather, it is fraught with a tender, little sadness that I'll come to feel more when I've finished the novel. How many times have I hesitated to save the novel to a CD! How many times have I felt a mixture of pride and relief after the achievement, mixed with that true regret for saying good-bye to the characters with whom I've lived two or three years!

Now it's time to leave. As soon as I hit "print," I will leave my friends, the characters. From now on thousands of readers will share my love for them. But there's no escaping that; this is life and such is the novel. The only solution to get over all that is to start thinking of a new novel.

TRANSLATED FROM THE ARABIC BY FAROUK ABDEL WAHAB

You have none of Pierre Michon's magisterial language, Echenoz's elegant reserve, or Houellebecq's powers of analysis. But if you take great care not to lose sight of who you are, you just might succeed in finding a way.

Don't "make" literature. Don't write because that's what people expect of you now that you're a "writer." Don't write for the beauty of the gesture or the love of art. Beware of fine phrases and well-turned maxims; that's not your thing. Watch out for words that strike a pose. But do let your memory and your instincts flow; let the aptest words, the words that resemble you most closely, come of their own accord. Call a spade a spade (you do it beautifully sometimes without even being aware of it). Write while it's still warm, before distance intervenes, before you allow yourself to be corrupted by your desire to please. And don't let yourself be misled by what editors, journalists, or readers might expect of novelists in general: *style, energy, provocation, audacity*. Forget all that, even your own recipes. Empty your mind and let come what may.

Let necessity come and find the courage to drop it if nothing does (and try to persuade yourself that maybe it isn't so bad, even if you don't believe a word of it).

Be alone in order to remain free. Alone in order to keep a clear head. What a privilege, what an incomparable stroke of fortune it is, to know how to listen to yourself.

(Hold on. I've just cribbed a bit of Pennac.)

TRANSLATED FROM THE FRENCH BY ARTHUR GOLDHAMMER

P

PARALIPOMENA | LYDIE SALVAYRE

Plural of paralipomenon (from the Greek *paraleipomena*). *Literally*: things cast aside, omitted, forgotten. *Colloquial equivalent*: junk. "That's a pile of junk."

It is the stuff of literature. *Example*: A Russian exile, locked up in a Nazi prison, thinks of only one thing upon his release: that his shoelaces be restored to him (quoted by Nina Berverova). This typically novelistic detail provides ideally fertile ground for growing paralipomena. Any sensible person (apart from writers) will pass right over such an insignificant item and get straight to serious matters.

The word *paralipomenon* is itself a paralipomenon. Forsaken among the forsaken. As good as dead. Left out of the French dictionary *Le Petit Robert* (where, on the other hand, you do find the equivalent of such words and locutions as junk, no way, chopped liver, give a shit, Qi, and fuck off). Never uttered by newscasters, who distrust rare, affected vocabulary, apparently favoring barbarisms, solecisms, and other forms of incorrectness.

Synonym: Nothing. Trifle. Piffle. Nonsense. Twaddle. Superfluity. Something negligible, easily done without. Whatever. Example: literature, sex, etcetera.

Religious: The Book of Paralipomena: title ascribed by the Septuagint and the Vulgate to the biblical books of Chronicles, which summarize the history of the world from Adam until the edict of Cyrus, which decreed the rebuilding of the Temple (a history that, to put it bluntly, no one could care less about). The Paralipomena of Jeremiah: title of the critical revision by the Greeks, published for the first time in 1868 by A. M. Ceriani in the *Monumenta sacra et profana.* It is a perfectly fitting title for this work, which can be considered as a complement to the book of Jeremiah, for indeed it reports several "omissions" regarding the prophet.

Historical: The *Paralipomena of the Second World War.* Having to do with the tiny omissions that once peppered the official record of the French Collaboration period, and which lasted into the 1970s. At regular intervals certain governments spawn paralipomena that bad types later turn into bestsellers.

Psychological: Things omitted or left unspoken, again called paralipomena, which can reemerge at any time with all their libidinal force, assuming an incongruous and often violent form (wars, riots, works of fiction, etcetera).

Literary: A word beloved of Alfred Jarry for the gloriously poetic reason that we are dismayed by its meaning even as we inexplicably take delight in the way it sounds. (Let us mention, in this regard, that Jarry's centenary could be included in the category of paralipomena: a glaring omission, inversely proportional to the triumph in the real world of his protagonist Ubu.)

Paralipomena: more than a key word, a shibboleth.

TRANSLATED FROM THE FRENCH BY JANE KUNTZ

PATHOS | ALBERTO GARLINI

There are three theological virtues—faith, hope, and charity—"but of these the greatest is charity." In literature charity is called pathos. Pathos is a technical term from Greek rhetoric: the ability to stir intense emotion and total participation on the aesthetic and affective levels. Pathos is the concept on which I build my idea of the novel. I seek the readers' empathy for the characters that I trot out. I myself live in total empathy with them. They are more alive than living people.

Pathos, for me, is a concept that is opposed to the postmodern aesthetic. Whereas irony, quotation, and free play with structure are preached within the context of an intelligent disengagement that creates a pact between reader and author—"let us amuse ourselves"—I seek a knowledge that is not rational but mimetic. I believe that knowledge—as recent studies on mirror neurons show—is developed through physical and emotional identification with other subjects, real or invented. I believe that empathy is a characteristic that is particular to man, and that it is the basis for every moral (even the more despicable ones). I believe that literature has always served to bind the community to its moral possibilities. When I write a novel I give voice to the victims, to those who see reality from a point of view that is different from the dominant one. The victim's point of view seems more authentic to me: it unveils the hidden violence.

My apologies for being so serious. In real life I think I am a very funny guy. But the world has changed ever since theorizing about the postmodern began. Precariousness, liquidity, violence, separation, and social inequalities demand that our words carry some weight. That they be able to rebuild something, provide direction for even a single person. And not get lost in empty games.

TRANSLATED FROM THE ITALIAN BY MICHAEL F. MOORE

PHANTOM | YING CHEN

According to *Le Petit Robert*:

1. a supernatural apparition of a dead person
2. that which only has the appearance of a person or a thing
3. a personage or a thing from the past, a haunting memory
4. chimera and illusion

Its origins: *fantauma* in Greek, *phantasma* in Latin

According to *Origins,* by Eric Partridge:

1. From the word *phantasma* are born not only "phantom" but also "fantasy" and its adjective "fantastic."
2. "Phantom" has another link, "Phaeton," a son of the sun abducted in disgrace by a four-wheeled chariot.
3. "Phantasia" is the cousin of "fantasy," sharing the same Greek source *phanein*: to manifest, to represent, to shine. In French, *phantasia* becomes "fantaisie" and its adjective "fantastique."
4. The Latin word *pantasiare*, a derivation of "phantasia": nightmare.

Translation of "phantom" in English:

1. Ghost: from Middle English *gastern*: to terrify; from Old English *gastlic*: soul and breath.
2. Specter: with a Latin ancestor *spectare*: element. A fertile word, one of whose descendants is the word "spectacle."

Translation of "phantom" in Chinese:

1. *Hun*: existence in the cloud
2. *Yu Lin*: intelligence in the shade

TRANSLATED FROM THE FRENCH BY YING CHEN

PHYSICAL | LUC LANG

Writing and reading, like speaking, are linked to the breath, to respiration, to the modulation of sounds, to melodic lines. It is undoubtedly due to the influence of American literature and of Conrad that I learned to love hearing the narrator and the narration breathe, and to breathe with them. The *physical* is essential for me in my work as a novelist.

When the action is rapid, exhausting, dizzying, I want the reader to feel in his or her body the speed, the effort, the breathlessness, the movement, the fatigue that the writing exudes. When the narrative turns peaceful, contemplative, or joyous, I want this condition to pervade the reader.

We need to bang into words just as we bang into objects, into a closed door, into a window frame. Ouch! That hurts! *Shit!* Can you feel the bump, right there, at the top of my head? There, put your finger on it. Words have a physical aspect that matches the physical aspect of life, of beings, and of things, a physical aspect that accompanies as much as it transforms. Words and their syntax are as much weapons that can kill as they are perfumes that can intoxicate.

When the reader opens one of my novels, I want him or her to enter into a carnal and concrete world where the senses are called upon just as much as the mind. I want this to be an experience the reader goes through and not simply a thought that he understands. I want the cerebrality, the sense that emerges, to be no more than a consequence of the senses.

Hence my satisfaction when readers of my 2006 novel *La Fin des paysages* [The Last Landscape] told me that this alcoholic quest, this febrile inquiry by a lost narrator, had left them breathless, drained, and disoriented.

TRANSLATED FROM THE FRENCH BY RORY MULLHOLLAND

PLAGUE | DAVID PEACE

To be honest or stupid or both, but not churlish or contrary
(I hope), I am uncertain I understand the premise of this
lexicon. However, I am against the presumption of all prem-
ises and, equally, I am against all definitions and diction-
aries, lexicons and lists, which, in their commodification
and exclusivity, are for me the preserve and the territory of
fascists and shoppers. So, under duress, I can only give you
the word that inspires and instructs me today, Wednesday,
6 February 2008, as I try to write a book called "Occupied
City." That word is Plague, and it was given to me by Daniel
Defoe, Edgar Allan Poe, Antonin Artaud, Sakaguchi Ango,
Albert Camus, Jean Genet, Paul Celan, Terayama Shuji, and
Heiner Müller, *among others, many, many others*. But that
word could also be Epidemic or Pestilence. Occupation or
Possession. Yesterday that word was Defeat, and tomorrow
that word might be Retreat—or Resistance (to the Plague, to
the Premise, always).

(THE) PRESENT | JEAN-YVES CENDREY

Since the advent of human societies or, better yet, since the
advent of humanity there has never been a lack of customers
at the old fart ticket window, which is open 24/7. True, the
tickets are handed out for free, and it's not hard to meet the
criteria for getting one.

Century after century writers have taken their place in
this line and duly received their ticket to moan about the past,
loathe the present, spit on the younger generation, shit on its

work, and piss on whatever they themselves do not produce; they are zealous censors and reactionary zealots who claim to be saving us from the apocalypse and who, in their charge backward, knock over mere lovers of the status quo.

They are at home with diktats and doctrines and are amazingly at ease among the vociferous backpedalers and the ill-tempered preachers of cultural hygiene. They are great champions of historical restoration and can be compared to costume buffs, devotees of greatcoats for *poilus* and SS officers; of Resistance fighters' berets and bicycles with messages, written in impeccable French, hidden in the handlebars; of broad-wale corduroy smelling of real French yokel and good smoke from our local oak burning in period fireplaces; devotees of exposed stone and equally exposed beams (except for those in their own eyes); of gray smocks and inkwells, of authentic, strict schoolmasters and the childhood terrors that go with them; devotees of the countryside and the far reaches of the countryside and the very farthest reaches of the countryside, where no one was afraid of hard work and village feuds could last a thousand years; devotees of Paris, capital of literary styles and stylishness—of a grafitti-free Paris, a rapless, slam-less Paris; devotees of good songs written by real lyricists; of their own books written with their smiling faces in the true, one and only manner; devotees of grammar books who nonetheless conjugate verbs exclusively in the past, and who even worship, as if it were the future, a more-than-past past tense of their own invention. They praise great men (they don't make them like that anymore) and great women (they don't make them like that anymore either) who strikingly resemble their dear, darling mothers. They worship the woodlands redolent of wild mushrooms, pen pushers of the old school, piles of tomb statuary and miles of lamentations. They praise the telegenic old wise men who drivel on like one knew how to drivel on in the good old days. Some of them are so stupid that they believe in God, and they all push their pathetic cult of the past to the point of praising one another.

You want names? Sorry, I don't have the time. So much the better. To hell with it all! Long live the present!

TRANSLATED FROM THE FRENCH BY ALYSON WATERS

R

"REAL" | PHILIPPE FOREST

Excerpt from the online article on *newwikipedia.com*. Last update: January 25, 2108. Automatic translation into English by the software Babel 2106. Document edited and transmitted by Philippe Forest.

. . .

To conclude, we can observe that the notion of "the Real"—as it was defined several decades earlier by the psychoanalyst *Jacques Lacan* (1901–1981)—enjoyed a modest and short-lived success in France among some writers whose works (mostly forgotten today) are nonetheless testimony to the profound crisis that French literature went through at the very end of the twentieth century. In his extensive survey of this question (*The French Novel, 1981–2057: Agony and Autopsy*, NewHarvardUniversityPress.com, 2073), *John W. Liang-Smith* (2030–2101) alludes to this phenomenon in a footnote: "To define the Real as impossible, thus showing allegiance to the thinking of *Jacques Lacan* and, more so, to that of *Georges Bataille,* represented a rather vain attempt to keep alive artificially the avant-garde theses that had led French literature to the dead end that we know, while making these theses compatible with an unacknowledged return to the old realism and its obsolete humanistic ambitions." Such a position, doubly archaic, was eventually condemned by the evolution of a literary field itself that would be dominated from then on, as *John W. Liang-Smith* also explains, by the invention of a new naturalism and the development of an aesthetic of "virtual worlds," advantageously attuned to the great cultural revolution that was starting at the time. In a footnote to another important study (*Houellebecq and After,* N.H.U.P.com, 2069), the author, recalling the hostile reactions provoked by the renewal of French literature, mentions as an example of the proponents of a poetics of the Real in the novel the case of Philippe Forest (1962–2035), author, between 1997 and 2007, of five novels and an essay in which he developed, in a systematic and rather insistent fashion, the idea that "the novel responds to the call of the Real, in other words, the impossible." We may draw satisfaction from the fact that such a regressive conception, going so clearly against the current of literary history, had no influence and no future whatsoever.

TRANSLATED FROM THE FRENCH BY PASCALE TORRACINTA

THE REAL | NICOLE MALINCONI

The real and not reality.

Reality is but a poor relative of the real. Yet it is where the real—that elusive thing—resides. Reality lets slip but a glimpse of what's inside it—and even then we must pay close attention—a glimpse, and nothing more. Not just what's inside it, but something else that, no longer having anything to do with it, still must be seen; the unnameable, something like the unnameable essence of all that is. If we could name it, grasp it, it would doubtless be unbearable. And yet trying to draw closer to it is an unceasing quest.

Throughout his life Giorgio Morandi painted the vases and the bottles he placed about his studio. The work of placing them took as much time and attention as the painting; these vases were precisely what he painted. And yet, or perhaps because of this, because of the gaze's attachment to the realness of these objects; because, one might say, of the gaze's anxiety over their mystery a kind of painting developed which, while faithful to the objects set about, transcended them, revealing about them something that could not be seen.

Michel Leiris once wrote of Francis Bacon: "This table here . . . is purely functional. Prosaic. The prosaic has no presence. Bacon takes this table and paints it so that it becomes obvious, so that it occupies, invades the room where we are" (M. Leiris, "Francis Bacon, or the Brutality of Fact").

And when he gazed on the sea or at soccer players Nicolas de Staël "saw," beyond their reality, a core beyond words: he painted this fleeting, unattainable presence of the real; in looking at it, we are astonished to find that "it is indeed" what we thought and yet we see in it, at the same time, something else we cannot put into words.

I think the same goes for writing. Writing lets itself be bumped about by whatever comes its way: facts, objects, lives. For me writing is letting the words happen, tugging them from the prosaic, letting them reveal themselves to me as vases did themselves to Morandi or the table itself to Francis Bacon. . . . Essential work, so that facts, objects, and lives remain bits and pieces of that which, without such work, I would have let slip away. To write just that: the certainty and uncertainty of this process.

TRANSLATED FROM THE FRENCH BY EDWARD GAUVIN

(HOLY) RUSSIA | GENEVIÈVE BRISAC

My wellspring! Where it all comes from. The modern novel owes her everything. My music owes her everything. Anton Chekhov and Isaac Babel, Fyodor Dostoevsky and Marina Tsvetaeva. Not forgetting Jossip (Joseph) Brodsky, the subtly mocking poet of *Flight from Byzantium*, now at rest in the Jewish section of the Venice cemetery.

I might equally have written "soul" instead of "Russia," the Slav soul, *kaniechno* [of course]. The Revolutionary Russia of our youth! *"Tchto dielats?"* ["What's to be done?"] said Vladimir Ilich Oulianov (aka Lenin), and the question being still apt I love to repeat it. When I say "Russia" I hear the joyous clamour of komsomols on the breathtaking shores of Lake Baikal, I can just make out the throaty singing of the sunflowers, those boundless hopes, the Black Sea, *tchornaia morie,* the scathing humour of a woman poet, walking bare-foot along the winding, sunken lanes of *russkaia polia* [the plain of Russia]. I breathe in the odor of lime trees and black-berry bushes. Russia. The chanting of the Slavonic monks of Novodievichy haunts my soul and cradles my pain. When I say "Russia" I hear the Song of the Marshes, the songs of the Partisans, I see the snow and the dead horses, a pair of fragile spectacles smashed on the ground. Abandoned railway carriages, a plume of smoke rising from each *isba* [log hut]. The witches' *isbas* on their hens' feet moving away across fields of frozen barley. *Dievuchki platchout.* The young women weep. I have by heart lullabies to console them. Russia, ah, Russia knows the meaning of consolation.

Literature decidedly belongs to the losing side: Russia and her Jewish emigrants, dispersing to the four corners of the Earth with their films, their poems, their books, and this thorn in their hearts—they embody it.

TRANSLATED FROM THE FRENCH BY J. A. UNDERWOOD

S

A SUCCESSFUL SENTENCE | GILA LUSTIGER

In my opinion, an author is the sum of the characters that inhabit his pages, and that includes the traitors, cowards, the bourgeois, education philistines, and the troublemakers. He must be able to embrace these characters in a cool, distanced, descriptive manner. He cannot remove himself from them or refer to them in disgust as "the others." That is the dangerous consolation of writing: being everyone apart from oneself.

There is, of course, something else at play too: the negation of any development. I have not simply become through a prolonged process of punishment, assimilation, renunciation, revolt, and compromise. I am my characters, things, and sentences. Whatever I find myself creating, my fountain pen hovering over the paper as I ponder the next word.

Everything I write is therefore autobiographical. And yet factually it is false; I am always having to lie. Not because there are things that ought to be covered with a veil of silence out of shame but because reality without some sort of aesthetic distortion is uninteresting. I even believe that reality captured in the hopelessly everyday language of reality is not in itself real.

It is not the biographical alone that counts; it is also every bit of reality that others attach to a person. The result is a tendency toward anonymity: look, understand, explore, and write.

If everything is material, then it is, as for the sculptor, a question of shaping that material, of shaving off layer by layer what is not necessary, of removing the anecdotal so as to make a scene more obvious, more present, more palpable.

I try to fix the moment in its constantly changing reality. Sometimes, as I scrunch up the page for the twentieth time, consider, and start again, I think that I'm like those gnats that keep bumping up against the lamp in summer.

A successful sentence, however, has an independent existence.

TRANSLATED FROM THE GERMAN BY REBECCA MORRISON

SHADOW | ELISABETTA RASY

Among the many possible cultural references to the word *shadow*, I single out the line from a poem by Paul Celan: "Speaks true who speaks shadow" [Wahr spricht, wer Schatten spricht].[1]

....

1. The line by Paul Celan is from the 1954 poem "Sprich auch du" (Speak you too). In his biography *Paul Celan: Poet, Survivor, Jew* (New Haven, Conn.: Yale University Press, 2001) John Felstiner writes that the verse, written in response to a review, is "as if the poet had been misheard and must tell himself to hold fast to the difficult way."—trans.

Shadow is an effect of light; in complete darkness there are no shadows: it is light which reveals shadow. Shadow can conceal what is often dangerous (the monster lurking in the shadows) or it can be restorative (cool, refreshing shade). Shadow is also that image of ourselves that is cast on the ground or on a wall and that, unlike us, changes dimension and shape—it may be elongated at certain hours of the day, or contracted, it can transform us into giants or make us regress to the trifling size of a child—an image that is not only more flexible than other possible portrayals but also more flexible than we ourselves are.

Shadow is also that dimness in which something that was visible in full light is then lost, whereas something else that was not visible in full light suddenly stands out and draws our attention. Moreover, in Italian an "ombra" indicates a slight quantity of a substance, or the shadow of a thought passing across a person's face.[2]

But in addition to shadow, which in the singular has something highly individual about it, there are shadows, the vast and multiform plural population of shades. They are not actually ghosts; they are the legitimate denizens of Hades available to anyone—Ulysses, Aeneas, Dante, to mention only the most prestigious visitors to that realm—who feels the need to consult with them. Sometimes to facilitate the

---

2. In Venice a small glass of wine is called an "ombra." The usage derives from the ancient custom of meeting to drink a glass of wine in the shade of the Campanile in Saint Mark's Square.—trans.

task, or to make it clear to those who do not want to understand that there really is a need for consultation, it is the shades themselves who travel about and, wandering around somewhat restlessly, come to be called ghosts. In actuality, shadows tend to speak only when questioned or in cases of strict necessity.

Another way shadow comes up in common parlance is in the expression "the side in shadow." There's a side to people that is in shadow and a side of history and of stories that is in shadow.

I like to tread among this diverse range of shadow when I write.

TRANSLATED FROM THE ITALIAN BY ANNE MILANO APPEL

SIGNED D.C. | DENNIS COOPER

One morning Popeye and Olive Oyl peel like decals from the TV and live in our world. Out here they're so weird-looking, thin and loud, their thoughts open to the world like postcards.

They spend their days at matinees. Evenings they stroll along the docks. Seeing his muscles, boys throw brawls instead of keggers. Girls diet to flimsiness in awe of her figure.

I launch a "Stop the Freaks" campaign. I stand on their front lawn day and night burning scrawls of them in effigy. They discombobulate, arguing for their lives in ancient punch lines.

One night Popeye finds Olive with her wrists torn, the walnut in her neck scratched completely into view. He scoops up her body like damp newsprint and shows me how little she was.

I like the lack of reach in their eyes. I like their clean, woody smell. I'd like to share their pain, but they can only make me smile. I am heavier than my constructions understand.

SILENCE | DAVID ALBAHARI

Silence is what writers dream to achieve when they begin writing. They know that words are not sufficient without silence, and they also know that silence speaks better than any single word. "Those who know," said Lao Tzu, "do not speak. Those who speak do not know." There is a similar saying in the Talmud: "Teach your tongue to say, 'I don't know.'" In other words, learn not to speak. Teach yourself silence. It doesn't matter that, from a scientific point of view, true silence can never be achieved. We can still dream about it. In that respect, silence is like love. Nobody knows what love really is, and yet we all keep falling in love, hoping that we will realize what true love is. In the same way we keep trying to go beyond words, to see the other side of language, hoping that then, and only then, will we be able to express everything. It is a lonely and desolate road, but there are people who have traveled along that road. Beckett, Bernhard, Wittgenstein. And John Cage was there while working on his silent composition 4'33" It is a marvelous piece of music, and all writers should learn to sing it. It should be sung at least two times a day, early in the morning and late in the evening. It should be sung with no thought on one's mind and it should be sung with no word on one's mind. It should be sung until one's whole being is empty and there is nothing but emptiness around it. It should be sung until the vision of the blank page appears. One should then take that page and read it slowly, enjoying its whiteness, savoring its silence. After all, if our world is really defined by our language, how beautiful and vast must be the world defined by our silence?

THE DEPOPULATED SKIES | THOMAS JONIGK

Stare down from above on the narrators of *Jupiter* and *40 Days*, massive, outsize, and difficult to discern: perceptible only as a dull rumbling, as darkness presaging rain, as a heavy cloud mass with rare glimpses of light, a boundary and a constant horizon, infinity and mortality in one; too large, too wide, too open to be immured within the regimented everyday world of work, habit, and diversion.

Below—down below—the earth is teeming, swarming with human beings, worker bees, soldier ants, sacrificial and innocent lambs, their thinking tirelessly turning on its own axis, sometimes attractive, sometimes uncouth, but always human and finite. The skies are reduced to a meteorologically relevant quantity where questions about the weather are answered. The weather in predictable dimensions, leaving aside hurricanes, tsunamis, a sweltering heat wave, or a biblical deluge. A blue sky is desirable for an afternoon walk; so is the horizon on a summer evening with the one you love beside you, or the starry firmament full of well-disposed planets: Uranus announcing change; the sun basking in its own success; Jupiter promising good fortune; and so on. In opposition to all of that stand free will and self-determination: the right to have rights. The right to be right. The right to freedom of action within the given possibilities. To understand abundance and variety as stress, responsibility as an excessive demand, omnipotence as impotence. Life as a one-way street to the grave, to your own funeral, where nothing may be expected but a deep hole dug in the ground: no profundity, only a sinking into the void, death and burial. And at the last moment, just before the coffin closes, your glance turns skyward: up to the skies depopulated by mankind itself, without what once gave them meaning, placed by humanity in human hands, and humanity finds its great power hard to bear. Ease, confidence, the sense of having a native land: none of that seems possible. Love, orgasm, the face of the beloved, everything that keeps momentarily coming between the ego and the void, promising a happy awakening after the daily nightmare of unbearable reality.

To put it differently, we can say with Emmanuel Lévinas: "To encounter a human being means to be kept awake by a mystery."

And we work so hard at solving the mystery that we reduce it to a problem.

TRANSLATED FROM THE GERMAN BY ANTHEA BELL

In Albanian the word *dhembje* (suffering) seems to be related to *dhëmb* (tooth). I imagine this word took on the meaning "suffering" from someone with a broken tooth. It reminds me of the horror I felt as a child every time I was dragged off to the dentist.

I don't know when I first began to experience literature as suffering. It may have been a period when I spent my time reading, before I began to write myself. I preferred the books of great writers, and there was certainly enough suffering in them. This universal literature of human suffering riveted my imagination. I envisioned the characters fashioned by these great writers in the reality of my own country, of course, in a different aspect yet essentially the same. Under particular circumstances human beings prove again and again that they are still rocked in a cradle of primitiveness and savagery. And this transformed me into a pessimist.

I often endeavor to overcome my pessimism by calling to mind the Four Noble Truths of Buddha on suffering. In the first he teaches his disciples "birth is suffering, aging is suffering, illness is suffering, death is suffering, union with what is displeasing is suffering, separation from what is pleasing is suffering, not to get what one wants is suffering." In the second truth he speaks of the origin of suffering. In the third he speaks of the cessation of suffering. In the fourth—which, to my mind, is the most significant of all—he reveals the way leading to the cessation of suffering. According to Buddha, this is the "eightfold path: right speech, right actions, right livelihood, right effort, right mindfulness, right concentration, right understanding, and right thoughts."

But are the teachings of Buddha really sufficient to overcome suffering? I continue to write to release myself from it, even though I am painfully aware that I will never be free of it.

TRANSLATED FROM THE ALBANIAN BY ROBERT ELSIE

T

TERROIR | ANNIE PROULX

Terroir is a word most often associated with viticulture, a word evoking complexities of place and time, geography, weather and climate. To me it also has meaning in the construction of fiction that connects a story to a particular place, a construction that ties the lives of characters to the natural world around them; the characters bear the same relation to a region as the grapes do to their vineyard.

I usually write about rural North American people, and I particularly like to set stories in periods of economic change against a backdrop of natural resources and the uses people make of them, whether Atlantic outport, prairie-grazing lands, spruce forest, or Louisiana bayou. The worlds of the characters display shifting values, the collapse of traditional ways, and the difficulties of adjusting to new situations. Just as grapevines are subject to the vagaries of weather and climate, so are the lives of the characters affected by forces they cannot control: weather and climate, as well as economic and political decisions made by strangers in distant cities. This half-recognized powerlessness often afflicts the characters with submissive resignation (mythologized as "toughing it out") and hopeful faith in a deity. And those humans and animals who came before, and whom we know only through archaeological evidence, still cause deep reverberations of the past which continue to sound in the fiction, if only faintly.

I am research-oriented, the result of years of reading history. Much of the background exploration—of prehistory, regional geography, geology, wind currents, wildlife behavior, plant species, and watercourses—that makes up the preparatory work for my fiction is not directly described in the stories. At a subterranean level of knowledge of past events it exerts certain forces on what the characters see, eat, and drink, what they do for work and pleasure, and even how they die. The stories fall out of study of the landscape and onto the page.

North America is a particularly rich setting for fiction: its continental shape, like a vast chanterelle, and its north-south trending mountain ranges create sharp delineations in seasons and sensitive responses to and amplification of global climate nuances. I am like an iron filing to the magnets of such ice and fire, autumnal sorrow, broken migrations.

U

UN- | JONAS HASSEN KHEMIRI

The fact is, I think we've started to drift apart, my dictionary and I. There was a time when we had so much in common: we had the same references; we spoke the same language; we could sit up night after night and giggle at funny words. But recently something has happened. Our relationship has become more strained. We meet sometimes, sit around in cafés, and try to find something to talk about. We ask how work's going. We comment on the weather (God, but it's cold!). We fill silences with the clearing of throats. We try not to think about how differently nowadays we define words like *colored* or *manly*. "But what about Un-?," I ask the dictionary. Maybe we can agree on that? The magic little prefix that turns the world inside out? The almost invisible little syllable that changes freedom to unfreedom, feeling to unfeeling, done to undone? The dictionary clears its throat and points out that

Un- is, in fact, a "first element denoting s.th. with /a/ contrary quality/ies in relation to what is indicated by the subsequent element." I call the dictionary a stupid berk.

I apologize. After a few minutes of silence, I say that all my writing has embodied a curiosity about dichotomies. An ambition to blur the edges that separate black from white, and an attempt to show how much world is contained between truth and untruth, shared and unshared, real and unreal. The dictionary doesn't agree. I try again.

Un- as in the difference between a novel and an unnovel. Where the novel is best at dramatic curves and slickly probing portraits of people, the unnovel is best at something different. Words that are not the same old familiar ones. Or words that are the same old familiar ones but have suddenly become unhinged. An unman walked down an unstreet and met an unwoman. A language that never allows the reader to switch off and read on automatic pilot. A language that activates without excluding. Or what do you say? The dictionary merely sighs. But I don't give in.

Un- as in never being satisfied with the language we have. Un- as in the realization of how difficult it is to communicate with people in a language you have invented yourself. Un- as in doubting whether you will ever succeed. Un- as in continuing to try even so. Un- as in suddenly launching yourself over a coffee table and transforming a dictionary into confetti.

TRANSLATED FROM THE SWEDISH BY LAURIE THOMPSON

All writing ultimately is a question of knowing, of what the author can impart to the reader: the novelists with his plots, his inventions; the journalist with his facts, his discoveries, his "story." But there is also the matter—I had almost written "problem"—of what the reader cannot know. In fiction this is a matter, for the author, of information that is either suppressed temporarily (Proust loves to withhold information, as, for instance, when he tells us quite late in the novel that there was, in fact, a baron de Crécy once married to Odette, and hence that her surname was not a "nom de cocotte") or willfully withheld. (Does Lily Bart, the heroine of Edith Warton's *House of Mirth,* commit suicide or does she die of an accidental overdose? The author never says and we will never be able to know.) In the case of nonfiction, the matter is more vexed because the universe that the text inhabits and from which it derives its reality is not limited to the mind of the creator, as is the case with fiction, but is concentric with the universe itself—with potentially everything there is to know. To be sure, we often don't know certain things in nonfiction texts for the same reason we often don't know them in fiction: because the author hasn't thought of putting them there, or because it suits his purpose to withhold them. But in nonfiction texts there is also the matter (I won't say "problem") of what the author himself cannot know—what he has been unable to learn, to discover, to find out even if it is, after all, something he'd like to be able to tell the reader. In an era characterized by an unprecedented access to vast quantities of information—yes, the Internet with its oceans of random facts and undigested data, the instantly accessible opinions and theories, but also the tell-all daytime television shows, the endless impulse to reveal, explain, account for oneself in public—the persistence of (and the willingness to acknowledge) the unknowable, the sheer and irreducible fact that there are some things that cannot be apprehended for our information, edification, or entertainment, is probably a good thing. Absence, after all, helps to define presence; one way we know what we have is to be conscious of what we don't have, what has been lost or cannot be found. So, too, with texts. One of the things that shapes every narrative is its boundaries, the white space of the un-narrated, the un-told, the unknowable on the other side of the story. Without those borders, without the tension between what gets said and what gets left out (for whatever reason), there could be no literature.

THE UNREAL | ARTHUR JAPIN

Reality already exists. What's the point of describing it one more time? The commonplace is all around. Why would you want to imitate it? What kind of challenge is truth? It is already there. Opt instead for something preposterous. Shape one of the impossibilities you've just snapped out of. Try to make your latest dream convincing and comprehensible for your audience and you'll give them something they could never have imagined themselves. Show them something no one would have thought possible! Surely astonishment, rather than recognition, is a greater reward for your efforts?

And yet some artists are still convinced that unless they create lifelike characters, who speak and act like real people, their viewers, readers, and listeners will not be able to identify and empathize with them.

But people don't identify with ordinariness. On the contrary! It is the extraordinary that appeals to them. Not the trivial but the extreme. Nobody actually resembles Medea or Mary Poppins, but everyone sees a part of themselves in them. Even people who didn't kill their children and don't fly by umbrella can imagine themselves in their place. This is how we feel what is happening to these characters: not because their emotions are commonplace but because they are extreme, improbable, or exaggerated. This is what people recognize deep within themselves. The further characters are from me personally, the more I want to know about them. The less clear they are, the more I strive to fathom them.

If you stopped a passerby on the street, showed him a very distinct, painstakingly drawn portrait of someone, and asked, "Is this you?" he would only give it a quick glance.

"No," he would answer, "that's not me. That's someone else." And then he would walk on.

But try showing him a vague, smudged, coffee-stained daub.

"Is this you?"

At first he grins and then he looks. He shrugs. Looks again. "Well, that nose, um, there is some kind of resemblance. And there's something about the eyes; how strange. . . ." He studies the picture more closely. "Very peculiar." He holds it at arm's length and rotates it ninety degrees. And again.

Before he can seek a likeness, he has to think about himself. And even if he eventually decides that he can't recognize any of his features in the portrait you have shown him, he will still walk on with a different image of himself than the one he had when you stopped him.

TRANSLATED FROM THE DUTCH BY DAVID COLMER

W

WAITING/ATTENTION | ANNE WEBER

To find a key word, a symbolic, emblematic word—what a
dream that would be! It would be a word that encapsulated
my aspirations and expectations, my sadness and my joy, my
amazement at the quince's hairy skin, the wash of the sky,
and the delicate pattern of the cyclamen's leaves. And since
everything would be contained in this single, essential word,
since it would express everything, I wouldn't need to write
anymore. And good riddance too!

In the meantime let us take two words that in French, if
not in English, come from the same Latin verb (*attendere*)
and, while they may not sum up my work, at least they indi-
cate what enables it to come about: waiting and attention.

Those who have found (mushrooms, words, or faith, as
the case may be) say it's best not to search. Or, at any rate,
not to search too actively, let alone aggressively. One should
do the opposite: distract oneself, turn one's gaze elsewhere,

to one side, follow the flight of a swift or an old man's steps, "rack one's brains" [se creuser la tête]—unblock one's mind, make an empty space, allow gaps.

From having sometimes found myself (not mushrooms or faith, though), I know how difficult it is to refrain from searching. It takes long hours of waiting, indecision, boredom, exasperation, presence, and hope. Hours in which one is mainly occupied in being attentive, letting things come, fighting against bad ideas or against ideas period, "rejecting inadequate words," and learning to recognize and welcome the right word, the right rhythm.

So writing, more than anything, is a matter of not writing. And of attentive waiting.

TRANSLATED FROM THE FRENCH BY WILL HOBSON

WOMAN | BENOÎTE GROULT

If I chose the word WOMAN, which—if one has any faith in logic and biology—ought to be the first word used to denote humanity in the order of its appearance on the scene, it is precisely because I have had such trouble finding my place as a human being and as a citizen in an exclusively male world.

Born in 1920, I taught Latin and French long before I had access to any citizenship, long before I was considered capable of voting. Indeed, judging by the place they have occupied in human history—whether in art, science, sports, or literature, and, of course, politics—the equality of the sexes and the emancipation of women seem to have been the only concepts that have succeeded in bringing together men of every persuasion and from every country.

But it is very difficult to develop oneself without a past, without any emblematic images, without any reference points or markers in History. The few women who did try were systematically condemned to oblivion, ostracized from society, burned as witches (Joan of Arc), sent to prison (Pauline Roland, Louise Michel), guillotined (Olympe de Gouges), or locked up in an insane asylum (Théroigne de Méricourt). Shattered in the name of what Germaine Tillon has called "the most massive survival of slavery in the world."

The Declaration of the Rights of Man and the Citizen is more than 150 years old, but in France the word *man* continues to stand for the human species. If I chose the word *woman* and if I campaign in the name of "human rights," it is to symbolize women's final accession to equality.

It is about time, 100 years after the birth of the grandmother of modern feminism: Simone de Beauvoir.

TRANSLATED FROM THE FRENCH BY MARJOLIJN DE JAGER

THE WORD *WORD* | LESLIE KAPLAN

in a word all the words
big word little word
give me a word
just one word?
a just word?
and I'll lift up the world

tous les mots tous les mondes

something almost nothing

a shush word a silent word

no word without silence

"grain upon grain, one by one, and one day, suddenly,
    there's a heap, a little heap, the impossible heap"

a word closed like a fist

a word open like a world

"world world vast world, if I were called Earl, it would be
    a rhyme, not a solution"

infinitive word definitive word

word me word ego me I am me and you you shut up

wanting to have the last word

thinking one can

"When I use a word," Humpty Dumpty said, "it means
    just what I choose it to mean, neither more nor less."
    "The question is," said Alice, "whether you can make it
    mean different things." "The question is," said Humpty
    Dumpty, "which is to be master—that's all."

period that's all

but we don't need to take orders from an egg

and since we're in 2008

and spring is coming

let's say it: anything goes, it's forbidden to forbid

not in actions but in words

one word opens all the others

all words are equal

words live together

linked

related

connected

through words

quiet and disquieted

tight and full

like words

and here and now for me

I word a three-letter word

like the word sap

like the word art

like the word May

TRANSLATED FROM THE FRENCH BY THOMAS C. SPEAR

"WORDS, WORDS, WORDS" | PÉTER ESTERHÁZY

And the rest is silence. I might have chosen *this* silence for my "heraldic animal," in which case 1,500 empty character spaces would follow. But that would not be *entirely* fair because—as I see it—all novels exist inside this silence, on the border between silence and speech, so it wouldn't be *uniquely* characteristic. I don't know whether, as the request put to me suggests, a thought or *idea* lies in the background of a novelist's work, for my own is tied to a singular experience, namely, that I have nothing to work with except words. I have no father, no mother, no loves, no children; I have nothing but words. And then I start building from the words backward: a father, a mother, feelings, and so forth.

Which is an exaggeration, of course.

But Flaubert encourages us (or, to be more precise, literature) to exaggerate.

"Mask." That, too, could serve as my key word. There's a connection between it and word-centricity, for if we ignore so-called reality (what is reality? I'd rather not go into that now, and not merely for lack of space) and construct the world from words while, philosophically speaking (shades of Kant), we do not give the whole thing due consideration; we're hoping against hope that we are also saying something about the world, in which case we can adopt as many masks as we wish, with no limit set upon our endeavors except—and that's no mean limit!—the words on the page.

I should have also said something about quotation marks because that's very much part of the key word.

I was given a free hand to write these lines in the genre of my choice, and as you see I chose the genre of unencumbered speech.

TRANSLATED FROM THE HUNGARIAN BY JUDITH SOLLOSY

WORK | RAFAEL CHIRBES

> CAESAR DEFEATED THE GAULS—DIDN'T HE AT LEAST HAVE A COOK WITH HIM? . . . THEBES OF THE SEVEN GATES—WHO BUILT IT? IN THE BOOKS THE NAMES OF THE KINGS APPEAR. / DID THEY HAUL THE BIG BLOCKS OF STONE?
>
> BERTOLT BRECHT

Carpenters, locksmiths, plasterers, bricklayers: at times I overhear them discussing their work in the bar. They comment on the difficulties they run up against, tell each other how they resolve them. In the meantime they build walls, hang doors, install taps, put up railings. If you pass by what a few months ago was just a piece of empty ground, you now discover a house is being built in which someone leans out the window and from whose inside there comes the sound of voices or music. They go on talking in the bar about whether they've done a good job or whether they've been obliged to turn in something slipshod. I envy them the possibility of working together, of being able to put their skills to the test. That which lasts, doesn't get covered in cracks, supports the action of water, fits just so, the door that doesn't yield.

Meanwhile I see myself flapping about among shadows, capable of nothing, empty for days on end. I miss those craftsmen's certitudes: to have the avatars of time as a witness. The months go by, of course, and what was nebulous starts to become suspicious. The chaos is put in order and after a while a messenger from the publisher brings me a book of several hundred pages that—don't ask me how—has surged up from the depths of the nebulousness that pervades me. Like the walls, the doors, and the taps, my book, too, is but a result of work. I know that a book doesn't have the solidity of a house, but in Moscow few houses remain of the ones that were around when Tolstoy was alive, and of Berlin's old Alexanderplatz, what would remain if it weren't for Döblin's book? I tell myself I can argue about the resistance of materials with the workers in the bar because a house and a book are expressions of the surprising inner toughness retained by that fragile human animal felled in some accident or other.

TRANSLATED FROM THE SPANISH BY PAUL HAMMOND

Y

YUSUF | SUHAYL SAADI

"Joseph, Yusuf, Yosef, Yosep, Josip, Iosephus, Giuseppe, Eòsaph, perfectly righteous, master of dreams, servant of God, grand vizier of yarns, the man in the well; through song you rise over the horizon, a giant figure in white. Yusuf, possessed of such beauty no being can gaze upon you and remain a stone. Yuya, builder of Memphis, Moon of Canaan, the Loved One of the razbin geddisseh, you render song agreeable even unto the wolf. I cast pebbles into the stream and watch as the water turns to a mirror of your visage."

And she saw that Joseph was rising from the snow as though from a blank page and that in one hand was a rod of gold and that he was cloaked in a ketonet that possessed the quality of silk and the ketonet was of many colors and each of the colors revealed a secret. And behind all secrets were the songs of the hod-carrier, Almalaak Jibraeel, the angelic savior of Yosef in the well, and the songs of the Karubiyyun and Seraphiel, of Hazrats Daoud, Sulaiman and their massed, jinn orchestras.

Guided by the Archangel Raphael, the arefeh sought out the dark well at the world's end, Giuseppe's Well that lies beyond the White Mountains in the place beneath the Pole Star, the well that some say is more like a dark cistern.

"I danced like a bear and sang like a monkey and in that City of a Thousand Days that had been built by Hazrat Yusuf, the great luminary of Misra, I told tales to the walls of the Crimson Church in the languages of termites, griffins, and salamanders. Alf-yaum, alf-yaum, alf-yaum . . . the lost dream of Iosephus."

Yusuf, the soul, the one who needs no key.

Z

ZORBY[1] | JAMES FLINT

The rainbow skein of gasoline on a puddle. The orange haze around sodium vapor lights when the mist descends. The glow of a single laptop screen in a darkened room. The hum of servers in a silent building. Cloud bellies lit by a city at dusk. The hollow tang of a basketball bouncing on a baking court. The shiver of heat above a hot exhaust. The yellow cyclops eyes of taxis lined up in a row. The hiss of a Eurostar pulling into the Gare du Nord. The crust of sand turned to glass by an exploding missile. The glint of curtain walls in the midday sun. The copper pathways of a microprocessor seen under a microscope. The traces of a thousand passenger aircraft on a traffic controller's plasma screen. The remorseless black of a fighter pilot's visor. The pixellated strain of a digital viewfinder in low light. Countless multicolored

1. Adjective invented by James Flint

plastic particles drifting on the tide. Iron scum left by a dead, receding sea. The electric lattice of Los Angeles laid out on the land. Tankers hugging the horizon northwest of the Philippines. Soldiers' boots, a menacing green, in night vision. The whine of a modem connecting to a network. The hush of bus wheels in the rain two streets away. The creak of rooks above the roofs of vacant buildings. The amber blink of a cell phone's light-emitting diode to let you know your lover's left a message. The celestial echo of aircraft overhead. The distant thrum of trucks and motorbikes. The rust of dried blood on the road beside a checkpoint. The carboned steel of burned-out homes and cars. The shadows thrown through window blinds by passing headlights. The countless lives lived alongside countless railway tracks. The metal taste on your tongue when you wake at 3 a.m. The astonishing waste, the overwhelming beauty, the pure incomprehensibility of our being in this world.

CONTRIBUTORS

DAVID ALBAHARI, born in Pec in 1948, is one of the most important novelists from the former Yugoslavia. He currently lives in Canada. His work is deeply rooted in questions of identity prompted by historical divisions and explores the complexity of emotions (guilt, fascination) and the links between individual and collective histories.

Gotz and Meyer, translated by Ellen Elias-Bursac (Harcourt, 2005)

TARIQ ALI was born 1943 in Lahore (then part of the British Empire). He studied in Pakistan and then at Oxford University. His opposition to the Pakistani military dictatorship led him into exile in Great Britain. He has been a major left-wing figure since the end of the sixties. He is the author of political and historical essays as well as two series of novels. He also works as an editor in London and writes for the theater and films.

The Duel: Pakistan on the Flight Path of American Power (Scribner, 2008)

CHRISTINE ANGOT, born in 1959, is a French novelist and playwright. She has made her life the subject of her novels since her very first book, *L'Inceste* (Livre de Poche, 2001). With courage and determination she tirelessly dissects the subject "I" in her novels. *Rendez-vous,* published in 2006 by Flammarion, was awarded the prix de Flore the same year.

Le Marché des amants (Seuil, 2008)

NELLY ARCAN, born in 1975, is from Quebec. Her first novel, *Whore,* was short-listed for the prix Fémina and the prix Médicis. With *Folle* (Seuil, 2004) and *À ciel ouvert* (Seuil, 2007) she continues her inquiry into the agonies of the female mind. She is also the author of *L'Enfant dans le miroir* (Marchand de feuilles, 2007).

Whore, trans. Bruce Benderson (Grove Press, Black Cat, 2004)

AYERDHAL was born in 1959. He writes science fiction novels constructed like complex pieces of machinery, often calling for extrapolations of new scientific realities. He leads his readers into heart-racing scenarios that challenge perceptions and the power structures of the media and politics.

Demain, une oasis (J'ai Lu, 2007)

ANDRÉ BRINK was born in 1935 in South Africa. His stance against the apartheid system hardened after 1968. In 1973 he wrote *Looking on Darkness* (William Morrow) but it was with *A Dry White Season* (Harper Perennial) that he gained international recognition, winning the prix Médicis étranger in 1980. Having lived in Paris, he was also a translator for Albert Camus.

A Fork in the Road: A Memoir (Harvill Secker, 2009)

GENEVIÈVE BRISAC was born in Paris in 1951. She has published seven novels, notably *Losing Eugenio*, *Petite* (Seuil, 1996), and *Week-end de chasse à la mère* (Seuil, 1999), which have been translated into more than ten languages. She is also the author of *52 ou la seconde vie* (L'Olivier, 2007) and several essays, including "La Marche du cavalier" and "Loin du paradis" (on Flannery O'Connor), all published by L'Olivier in 2002.

Losing Eugenio, trans. J. A. Underwood (Marion Boyars, 2000)

A.S. BYATT was born in 1936 in Sheffield, England. She found fame with her novel *Possession* (Random House, 1990), for which she won the Booker Prize in 1990. Her stories reveal spellbinding writing that, far from distancing us from reality, invites us to look differently at the world around us.

The Children's Book (Knopf, 2009)

JAMES CAÑÓN was born and raised in Colombia. After having studied advertising at Jorge Tadeo Lozano University in Bogota, he moved to New York and started to write. He has published short stories in many different magazines and journals. *Tales from the Town of Widows* is his first novel.

Tales from the Town of Widows (Harper Collins, 2007)

JEAN-YVES CENDREY, born in Nevers in 1957, is the author of more than ten books, notably *Les Morts vont vite* (P.O.L), *Oublier Berlin* (P.O.L, 1994), *Les Jouissances du remords* (L'Olivier, 2007), *Les Jouets vivants* (L'Olivier, 2005), and *Corps enseignant* (Gallimard, 2007).

La Maison ne fait plus crédit (L'Olivier, 2008)

UPAMANYU CHATTERJEE was born in India in 1959. In 1998 he was appointed director of the Bureau des langues at the Ministry of Development and Human Resources. He has been awarded the prize for the English-language novel from the Académie Nationale des Lettres in 2004 for *The Mammaries of the Welfare State* (Viking, 2000). He is also the author of *English, August: An Indian Story* (Rupa & Co., 1989), his best-selling novel, which was later made into a major film.

Way to Go (Penguin Books, India, 2010)

YING CHEN was born in China in 1961. She writes in French and lives in Canada. In an attempt to distance herself from the pains of exile, her first novel, *La Mémoire de l'eau* (Lemeac, 1992), is a troubling immersion in contemporary China, seen through the eyes of women spanning several generations. With *Le Mangeur*, her latest novel, she focuses on the figure of the father, after having analyzed that of the mother in *Ingratitude* (University of California Press, 1999).

Le Mangeur (Seuil, 2006)

RAFAEL CHIRBES was born in Spain in 1949. After having studied history, he turned to journalism and literary criticism. He is the author of *La caida de Madrid* (Anagrama Edito 2006), *La larga marcha* (Anagrama Edito, 2006) and *Mimoun* (Anagrama Edito, 1988, short-listed for the Herralde Prize), among others.

Los Viejos Amigos (Anagrama, 2008)

HÉLÈNE CIXOUS was born in Oran, Algeria, in 1937. A novelist and essayist, she was awarded the prix Médicis in 1969 for *Inside* (Schocken, 1986). She has published much of her work with Des Femmes and Galilée. She regularly works with Ariane Mnouchkine's Théâtre du Soleil.

Love Itself: In the Letter Box (Polity, 2008); *Dream I Tell You* (Columbia University Press, 2008)

KAREN CONNELLY was born in Canada in 1969. She spent two years living on the border between Thailand and Myanmar among exiles, dissidents, and resistance fighters opposing the Myanmar dictatorship. Their testimonies supplied the material for her book *The Lizard Cage* (2007), for which she was awarded the Kiriyama Prize in 2006 and the Orange Broadband Prize for a first novel in 2007.

The Lizard Cage (Bantam Dell, 2007)

DENNIS COOPER was born in the United States in 1953 and now lives in Paris and Los Angeles, where he works as a journalist and arts critic. In 1985 he started a sequence of five novels called the *George Miles Cycle*. He is also the author of *Wrong* (Grove Press, 1994), *My Loose Thread* (Canongate, 2003), *The Sluts* (Da Capo Press, 2005), and the highly acclaimed *God, Jr* (Grove Press, Black Cat, 2005).

Smothered in Hugs: Essays, Interviews, Feedback, and Obituaries (Harper Perennial, 2010)

GIUSEPPE CULICCHIA was born in Turin in 1965. As a writer who belongs to another time, he takes great pleasure in destroying all the fantasies and little pleasures of his contemporaries. This young novelist highlights the perverse indoctrinations of modern society. Destroyer of bar codes, TV shows, and the reign of capitalism, he depicts with humor characters devoured by this absurd reality. He is the author of *Torino è Casa Mia*

(Laterza, 2006), *Il Paese delle Meraviglie* (Garzanti, 2006), and *Ambarabà* (Garzanti, 2002).

Brucia la Città (Mondadori, 2009)

CHLOÉ DELAUME was born in Paris in 1973. A guardian of free spirits, in her numerous literary works (novels, performances, Web sites) she dissects the personal and public spheres with incisive prose and powerful poetry.

Dans ma maison sous terre (Seuil, 2009)

ERRI DE LUCA was born in Naples in 1950. He is a columnist *for Il Manifesto* and a novelist whose work has been translated into seven languages. He lives outside Rome. *Montedidio*, published in English as *God's Mountain*, was awarded the prix Femina étranger in 2002.

God's Mountain, trans. Michael F. Moore (Riverhead, 2002)

MARIE DESPLECHIN was born in 1959. In *La Vie sauve* (Seuil, 2005), with Lydie Violet, she makes words of friendship speak as we have never heard them before. They are simple, sensitive, and vital. Their magnificent chronicle was awarded the prix Médicis Essai (2005). After writing children's books, in 1996 she started writing for adults, publishing *Taking It to Heart*, translated from the French by Will Hobson (Granta Books, 2001). Since then she has published a number of collections of short stories and novels, all of which are characterized by writing that is clear and committed.

Sans moi, trans . Will Hobson (Thomas Dunne Books, 2001)

ROBERT DESSAIX was born in Sydney in 1944. He is one of the emblematic figures of Australian literature. Since childhood he has been passionate about Russian literature and has consequently become one of its most eminent translators. He started writing after discovering that he is HIV-positive.

Twilight of Love: Travels with Turgenev (Counterpoint, 2005)

RIKKI DUCORNET was born in New York in 1943. She has lived in North Africa, South America, France, and Canada and now resides in the United States. Ducornet is both a painter and the author of novels, short stories, and poems. Her baroque writing is rich and extremely sensual, inspired by the fantasy and cruelty of fairy tales. The reader is transported into a sweet and carnal reverie at the heart of the private and subversive territories of reading and the imagination.

The One Marvelous Thing (Dalkey Archive Press, 2008)

DUONG THU HUONG was born in Vietnam in 1947. She was imprisoned in 1991 for having defended her democratic beliefs. She is the author of a number of books, notably *Paradise of the Blind* (Penguin Books, 1994) and *Myosotis* (Philippe Picquier, 2001). She remained under house arrest in Vietnam until January 2006, when she moved to Paris at the time of the publication of *No Man's Land*.

No Man's Land, trans. Nina McPherson and Phan Huy Duong (Hyperion, 2006)

RACHID EL DAÏF, born in Lebanon in 1945, is professor of Arabic language and literature at the University of Beirut. Although he started off writing poetry, he has been writing novels since the eighties. He is the author of *Passage to Dusk* (University of Texas Press, 2001), *Dear Mr. Kawabata* (Quartet Books, 2000*)*, and *This Side of Innocence* (Interlink Books, 2001).

Learning English, trans. Paula Haydar and Adnan Haydar (Interlink Books, 2007)

ALAA EL ASWANY was born in 1957. Son of a lawyer and a writer, he became a dentist and a novelist. He is the author of *The Yacoubian Building: A Novel* (Harper Perennial, 2006), which was later made into a film. Just like Naguib Mahfouz, he describes an Egypt that is both lively and open-minded, cruel and conservative.

Chicago: A Novel (Harper, 2008)

PÉTER ESTERHÁZY was born in Budapest in 1950. A descendant of the counts of Esterházy de Galántha, he is best known for *Celestial Harmonies* (2004) in which he retraces the journey of his ancestors under the Austro-Hungarian Empire until its decline under communism. He has been awarded numerous Hungarian literary prizes and was made the commander of the French Ordre des Arts et des Lettres in 1998.

Not Art: A Novel, trans. Judith Sollosy (Ecco, 2010)

MONIKA FAGERHOLM was born in 1961. She is Finnish but writes in Swedish. She has received a number of distinctions in Sweden, notably the August Prize. *Wonderful Women by the Water* (Harvill Press, 1998) was the first of her novels to be translated into English. *The American Girl* (2009) examines the agonies of adolescence against the background of the violence of class relations.

The American Girl, trans. Katherine E. Tucker (Other Press, 2009)

NURUDDIN FARAH was born in Somalia in 1945. He has lived in political exile since 1972 and divides his time between England and South Africa. He is the author of several books, including *Secrets* (Penguin Books, 1999), *Yesterday, Tomorrow: Voices from the Somali Diaspora* (Cassell, 2000), and *Links* (Riverhead, 2003).

Knots (Riverhead, 2007)

NICOLAS FARGUES was born in 1972. He grew up in Cameroon, Lebanon, and Corsica. He worked for the Alliance Française in Madagascar from 2002 to 2006. He is the author of *Le Tour du propriétaire* (P.O.L, 2000), *Demain si vous le voulez bien* (P.O.L, 2001), *One Man Show* (Gallimard, 2002), *Rade Terminus* (Gallimard, 2006), and *I Was Behind You* (2009).

I Was Behind You, trans. Sue Rose (Pushkin Press, 2009)

ALAIN FLEISCHER, born in Paris in 1944, studied linguistics, anthropology, and animal biology before dedicating himself to film, sculpture, photography, and writing. He he author of *Les Trapézistes et le rat* (Seuil, 2001), *Mummy, mummies* (Verdier, 2002), *La Hache et le violon* (Seuil, 2004), *La Femme couchée par écrit* (Léo Scheer, 2004), *Immersion* (Gallimard, 2005), *L'Accent, une langue fantôme* (Seuil, 2005), and *L'Amant en culottes courtes* (Seuil, 2006).

Le Carnet d'adresses (Seuil, 2008)

JAMES FLINT, born in 1968, is a leading voice in British literature. Brought up on comic books, science fiction, new technology, and Russian literature, he is the author of three exhilarating novels. At the crossroads between technoscience, psychology, and philosophy, his novels explore the impact of new technology on our lives and the world today.

The Book of Ash (Penguin Books, 2005)

PHILIPPE FOREST, born in Paris in 1962, is professor of literature at the University of Nantes. He is an essayist, a critic for *Art Press,* and the author of numerous essays dedicated to the avant-garde (such as *Histoire de Tel Quel* [Seuil, 1995]). He is the author of *L'Enfant éternel* (1998), which won the prix Femina du premier roman; *Toute la nuit* (1999), winner of the prix Grinzane Cavour; and *Le Nouvel Amour* (2007)—all published by Gallimard.

Sarinagara, trans. Pascale Torracinta (Mercury House, 2009)

RODRIGO FRESÁN was born in Buenos Aires in 1963 and now lives in Barcelona. Writer, journalist, and a leading figure in the Latin American literary revival, he is the author of *Esperanto* (Tusquets Editores, 1997) and *Kensington Gardens* (2006).

Kensington Gardens, trans. Natasha Winmer (Faber and Faber 2006)

ALBERTO GARLINI was born in Parma in 1969. After studying law, he quickly turned to writing of all kinds, including poetry, literary criticism, and novels. He also organizes the Pordenonelegge Festival and contributes to the cultural pages of *Giornale* and *Messaggero Veneto.*

Futbol Bailado (Sironi, 2004)

BENOÎTE GROULT, born in 1920, is the author of more than fifteen novels. She has contributed to *Elle* magazine and is the author of *Salt on Our Skin* (Hamish Hamilton, 1991) and *Desire* (Avon Books, 1994). Now in her late eighties, she continues to write on a variety of issues.

Mon évasion: autobiographie (Grasset, 2008)

KIRSTY GUNN was born in 1960 in New Zealand. She has worked as a journalist in New York and London and now teaches creative writing at the University of Dundee in Scotland. Her latest books include *The Boy and the Sea* (Text Pub. Co., 2006), winner of the 2007 Sundial

Scottish Arts Council Book of the Year Award, and *44 Things: My Year at Home* (2007).

    44 Things: My Year at Home (Atlantic Books, 2007)

YANNICK HAENEL was born in 1967. He is the author of *Les Petits Soldats* (La Table Ronde, 1996), *Introduction à la mort française* (Gallimard, 2001), *Évoluer parmi les avalanches* (Gallimard, 2003), and *À mon seul désir* (Argol, 2005). He is also coeditor of the journal *Ligne de risque*.

    Prélude à la délivrance (Gallimard, 2009)

JACQUES HENRIC was born in Paris in 1938. He published his first novels in the collection *Tel Quel* and has contributed to *Lettres françaises*. He works for *Art Press* and is the author of numerous novels and essays, including *Peinture et le mal* (Grasset, 1983), *Légendes de Catherine M.* (Denoël, 2001), and *Comme si notre amour était une ordure* (Stock, 2004).

    Politique (Seuil, 2007)

CHRISTOPHE HONORÉ, born in 1970, is a film director, children's book author, screenwriter, and film critic. In 1997 he published his first book for adults, *L'Infamille* (L'Olivier, 1997). *Scarborough* (L'Olivier, 2002) and *La Douceur* (L'Olivier, 2005) soon followed. He is director of the films *Dans Paris* and *Les Chansons d'amour*. His latest movie, *La Belle Personne*, is a contemporary adaptation of *La Princesse de Clèves*.

    Le Livre pour enfants (L'Olivier, 2005)

HWANG SOK-YONG was born in 1943 in Manchuria, where his family had taken refuge to avoid Japanese colonization. His work, deeply anchored in historical reality, constitutes a vibrant political commentary. His latest novel is strongly autobiographical and retraces the journey of a generation of Koreans inspired by the utopian ideals for which he fought. It has been made into a film by Im Fang-Soo.

    The Old Garden, trans. Jay Oh (Seven Stories Press, 2009)

ARTHUR JAPIN, was born in Haarlem, Holland, in 1956. In addition to writing, he has been an actor and an opera singer. His first novel, *The Two*

Hearts of Kwasi Boachi (Vintage, 2002), received international acclaim, and *In Lucia's Eyes* was awarded the Libris Prize.

In Lucia's Eyes, trans. David Colmer (Knopf, 2005)

THOMAS JONIGK was born in Eckernförde, on the Baltic Sea, in 1966. He became well known in Germany and Austria as a playwright, director, and librettist, later provoking much debate and controversy with his first novel, *Jupiter* (Residenz Verlag, 1999).

Vierzig Tage (Droschl, 2006)

LESLIE KAPLAN was born in New York in 1943 and has lived in Paris since early childhood. Trained in philosophy, history, and psychology, she is a politically committed writer. Whether she is writing about her experience as a factory worker in *L'Excès—L'Usine* (P.O.L), her first book, or of her experience with psychoanalysis in *Le Psychanalyste* (P.O.L), her writing leads the reader to question the world we live in.

Brooklyn Bridge (Barrytown Limited, Station Hill Press, 1992)

ETGAR KERET was born in Israel in 1967. Novelist, cartoonist, and film director, he is the author of several works, including *"The Bus Driver Who Wanted to Be God" & Other Stories* (Thomas Dunne Books, 2001) and *The Girl on the Fridge: Stories* (Farrar, Straus, and Giroux, 2008). As screenwriters and directors, he and his wife, Shira Geffen, won the 2007 Palme d'Or for Best Debut Feature (*Jellyfish*) at the Cannes Film Festival. His latest book, *Pipelines,* was published in France by Actes Sud in 2008.

Pizzeria Kamikaze (Alternative Comics, 2007)

JONAS HASSEN KHEMIRI was born in 1978 to a Tunisian father and a Swedish mother. He grew up in Stockholm, studied economics in Paris, and has worked for the United Nations. He received the most important Swedish prize for a first novel for *Ett öga rött (*Pan/Norstedt, 2003*). Montecore: En Unik Tiger* also led him to be nominated "Best Novelist of the Year" by the daily newspaper *Stockholm City*.

Montecore: En Unik Tiger (Dagensbok, 2006)

FATOS KONGOLI, born in 1944 in the central Albanian town of Elbasan and raised in the capital of Tirana, is one of the most forceful and convincing contemporary Albanian novelists. As a young man he studied mathematics in China during the tense years of the Sino-Albanian alliance. Unlike other novelists, Kongoli remained in Albania, though he also kept his silence. His narrative talent and individual style emerged in the nineties, following the fall of the Communist regime. His telling and powerful narratives exposed the crimes it had visited upon the Albanian population.

The Loser, trans. Robert Elsie and Janice Mathie-Heck (Seren, 2008)

DANY LAFERRIÈRE, born in Port-au-Prince, Haiti, in 1953, emigrated to Quebec in 1976. *How to Make Love to a Negro Without Getting Tired,* translated by David Homel (Coach House Press, 1987), had international success and was made into a film by Jacques Benoît in 1989. Notable among his publications are *A Drifting Year* (Douglas & McIntyre, 1997) and *Down Among the Dead Men* (Douglas & McIntyre, 1997). He is also a journalist and scriptwriter.

Je suis un écrivain japonais (Grasset, 2008)

LUC LANG was born in 1956. He has lived in Italy, Africa, and Japan. He is a professor and teaches aesthetics at the École nationale supérieure d'Arts de Cergy-Pontoise. Apart from his novels, he has also published numerous articles on contemporary art in exhibition catalogues, edited collections, and scientific reviews.

Strange Ways, trans. Rory Mulholland (Orion, 2002)

JONATHAN LETHEM was born in New York in 1964. First considered a genius of New Wave science fiction for such novels as *As She Climbed Across the Table* (Doubleday, 1997), he earned renown for *Motherless Brooklyn* (Doubleday, 1999), for which he was awarded the National Book Critics Circle Award, among others.

Chronic City (Doubleday, 2009)

GILA LUSTIGER was born in Germany in 1963. After studying literature at the Hebrew University of Jerusalem, she moved to Paris, where she has been living and working since 1988. Her novels are renowned in Germany and have been applauded by French critics. In her latest book, *Nous sommes* (Stock, 2005), an intimate historical and familial novel, Lustiger collects her memories together in an attempt to capture an elusive truth about her father, a survivor of Auschwitz.

The Inventory, trans. Rebecca Morrison (Arcade, 2001)

NICOLE MALINCONI, despite her Italian roots, was born in Wallonia in 1946 and lives in Belgium. Her experience as a social worker inspired her novel *Hôpital silence* (Minuit, 2002), an account of an abortion in a hospital environment. She won the prix Rossel for *Nous deux* (Eperonniers Belgique, 1993). *Vous vous appelez Michelle Martin* (2008) is based on an interview with Marc Dutroux's wife.

Vous vous appelez Michelle Martin (Denoël, 2008)

COLUM MCCANN was born in Dublin in 1965 and now lives in New York. He is the author of many short stories and novels. His works of fiction, often marked by the brutality of exile and exclusion, are characterized by precise and vivid writing that allows him to describe a topography of violence and to bring out the experience of marginality (whether in Ireland or in the United States).

Let the Great World Spin (Random House, 2009)

JAMES MEEK was born in London in 1962. Novelist, short story writer, journalist, and reporter, he lived in Russia from 1991 to 1999. He has been awarded prestigious international prizes for his reporting on Iraq and Guantanamo Bay. One of his novels, *The People's Act of Love* (Canongate, 2005), is a striking portrait of Russia in 1919 as it was descending into chaos.

We Are Now Beginning Our Descent (Canongate, 2008)

DANIEL MENDELSOHN, born on Long Island, New York, in 1960, studied classics at Princeton and the University of Virginia. He writes regularly for the *New York Review of Books* and the *New York Times Magazine. The Lost: A Search for Six of Six Million* (HarperCollins, 2007) earned him two literary prizes: the National Jewish Book Award and the National Book Critics Circle Award.

How Beautiful It Is and How Easily It Can Be Broken (HarperCollins, 2008)

PASCAL MERCIER was born in Bern, Switzerland, and currently lives in Berlin, where he is a professor of philosophy. *Night Train to Lisbon* (2008) is his third novel and his first to be published in English.

Night Train to Lisbon (Atlantic Books, 2008)

RICK MOODY, born in New York in 1961, grew up in the suburbs of Connecticut, which would become the privileged setting for his novels. His America, characterized by vacuity and cynicism, is crumbling. *Demonology* (Back Bay Books, 2002), *The Black Veil: A Memoir with Digressions* (Back Bay Books, 2003), and *The Diviners* (Little, Brown, 2005) earned him notoriety in France.

The Four Fingers of Death (Little, Brown, 2010)

LUDMILA OULITSKAÏA was born in 1943 in the southern Urals and lives in Moscow. Also known for her plays and films, *Mensonges de femmes* (2007) is her eighth book to be translated into French. She is the author, among others, of *Sincèrement vôtre, Chourik* (Gallimard, 2005), *Le Cas du docteur Koukotski* (Gallimard, 2003), *"Un si bel amour" et autres nouvelles* (Gallimard, 2003), and *Médée et ses enfants* (1998).

Mensonges de femmes (Gallimard, 2007)

DAVID PEACE was born in Yorkshire, England, in 1967. His youth was marked by the crimes of the Yorkshire Ripper, who is the subject and inspiration for his black tetralogy. In 1992 he left the United Kingdom for Tokyo, where he still lives today. He is currently working on a trilogy about the city between 1946 and 1949.

Occupied City (Knopf, 2010)

ANNIE PROULX was born in Connecticut in 1935. She received the PEN/ Faulkner Award in 1992 for *Postcards* (Scribner, 1992), followed by the Pulitzer Prize and the National Book Award for *The Shipping News* (Scribner,

1993). Next she wrote *Accordion Crimes* (Fourth Estate, 1996); *Brokeback Mountain* (Scribner, 1997), which inspired the film by Ang Lee; and *That Old Ace in the Hole* (Scribner, 2002).

Fine Just the Way It Is: Wyoming Stories 3 (Scribner, 2008)

ELISABETTA RASY was born in France in 1947 and currently lives in Rome. Writer, journalist, and specialist in women's literature, her latest novel places Nadejda and Osip Mandelstam, the poet, in Russia in the middle of the civil war. Behind these extremely sensitive portraits, Elisabetta Rasy explores the Russia of the 1930s and, with much finesse, describes the distress of an entire generation of artists ground down by history.

La Scienza degli Addii (Rizzoli, 2005)

ERIC REINHARDT was born in Nancy, France, in 1965 and currently lives and works in Paris. He is an editor of art books and the author of *Demi-sommeil* (Actes Sud, 1998), *Le Moral des ménages* (Stock, 2002), and *Existence* (Stock). His latest book, *Cendrillon* (2007), was very successful in France.

Cendrillon (Stock, 2007)

OLIVIA ROSENTHAL was born in Paris in 1965. She is the author of five works of fiction published by Verticales, notably *Dans le temps* (1998), *Puisque nous sommes vivants* (2000), *L'Homme de mes rêves* (2002), and *Les Fantaisies spéculatives de J. H. le sémite* (2005). She has also written a play entitled *Les Félins m'aiment bien* (Actes Sud–Papiers, 2004).

On n'est pas là pour disparaître (Verticales, 2007), winner of the prix Wepler Fondation La Poste

SUHAYL SAADI was born in Yorkshire, England, in 1961 and practices medicine in Glasgow. He has worked for the BBC, the British Council, and the Scottish Council for many years. He has won numerous literary prizes for his short stories, poems, and plays. He is the author of *Psychoraag* (Black & White, 2004) and *The White Cliffs* (2006).

The White Cliffs (Sandstone Press, 2006)

LYDIE SALVAYRE, born in 1948 to an Andalusian father and a Catalan mother who settled in France in 1939, is a psychiatrist and novelist. Armed with the incandescence of language and the jubilatory power of words, she leads a masterful, corrosive, and determined struggle against deception and the forbidden, against the blandness and morbid halfheartedness of accepted thought.

Portrait of the Writer as a Domesticated Animal, trans. William Pedersen (Dalkey Archive Press, 2007)

ELIF SHAFAK was born in Turkey in 1971. She is the author of *The Saint of Incipient Insanities* (Farrar, Straus, Giroux, 2004), *The Gaze* (Marion Boyars, 2006), *The Bastard of Istanbul* (Viking, 2007), and *The Flea Palace* (Marion Boyars, 2007). Elif Shafak's works are deeply rooted in the fight for Turkish women's rights, where Islam and democratic, occidental values coexist. As an outspoken intellectual and activist, she continues to write for various daily and monthly Turkish publications.

The Forty Rules of Love: A Novel of Rumi (Viking, 2010)

ZERUYA SHALEV was born in a kibbutz in Galilee, Israel, in 1959. She lives and works as an editor in Jerusalem. From her very first novel Zeruya Shalev has picked apart the family unit and its numerous emotional conflicts with determination and a fastidious attention to detail.

Husband and Wife, trans. Dalya Bilu (Grove Press, 2003)

PETER STAMM was born in Switzerland in 1963. After studying commerce, he studied English, psychology, psychopathology, and accounting. He has spent much time in Paris, New York, and Scandinavia. Since 1990 he has been a journalist and writer. He has also written a radio play and a play for the theater. In 1997 he became chief editor of the magazine *Entwürfe für Literatur*. In 1998 he was awarded the Rauriser Literaturpreis for his first novel, *Agnès* (Bourgois, 2000). He currently lives in Winterthur, Switzerland.

On a Day Like This, trans. Michael Hofmann (Other Press, 2008)

TARUN J. TEJPAL, born in 1963, is a journalist, book reviewer, and essayist. He has worked for such publications as *India Today*, *The Paris Review*, *The Guardian*, *The Financial Times* (London), and founded the Indian national weekly *Tehelka*. In 2001 *Businessweek* declared him among fifty leaders at the forefront of change in Asia.

The Story of My Assassins (HarperCollins, 2008)

ADAM THIRLWELL was born in 1978 and grew up in the north of London. He was placed on *Granta*'s 2003 list of "Best Young British Writers" under forty. He is assistant editor of the literary magazine *Areté* and a fellow of All Souls College, Oxford. His first novel, *Politics* (Jonathan Cape, 2003), was widely acclaimed by the critics. His latest book, *Miss Herber* (2007), is an essay on translation.

The Escape (Farrar, Straus, and Giroux, 2010)

LYONEL TROUILLOT was born in 1956 in Port-au-Prince, Haiti, where he still lives today. In *Street of Lost Footsteps*, translated from the French by Linda Coverdale (Bison Books, 2003), *Thérèse en mille morceaux* (Actes Sud, 2000), or *Bicentenaire* (Actes Sud, 2004) Trouillot speaks with the voice of opposition, which, like him, is committed to fighting for the democratic construction of his country. With his latest text, *L'Amour avant que j'oublie* (Actes Sud, 2007), he reveals the intimate.

Children of Heroes, trans. Linda Coverdale (University of Nebraska Press, 2008).

ADRIAAN VAN DIS was born in Holland in 1946. His stories are inspired by his travels. His latest tale is structured around the story of a family haunted by a painful colonial past. With a caustic sense of humor and a streak of cruelty, Van Dis depicts extremely colorful characters who often straddle the grotesque and the fantastic.

Repatriated, trans. David Colmer (William Heinemann, 2008)

DIMITRI VERHULST was born in Belgium in 1972. He began his career as a writer in 1999 with a collection of short stories. Since then he has written two novels as well as a collection of poems entitled *Liefde, tenzij anders vermeld* (Nederlandstalig, 2001), which was short-listed for the Buddingh Prize. He also writes for the Flemish daily *De Morgen*.

Problemski Hotel, trans. David Colmer (Marion Boyars, 2004)

PHILIPPE VILAIN was born in 1970. Since his first novel, *L'Étreinte* (Gallimard, 1997), he has been the main subject of his books, seeking to bear witness to intimate experience. He explains himself in *Défense de Narcisse* (Grasset, 2005) and his love life in *Paris l'après-midi* (2006). His books are like poetic acts, seeking to explore love, the body, and the flesh.

Paris l'après-midi (Grasset, 2006)

ENRIQUE VILA-MATAS was born in Barcelona in 1948. At the age of eighteen he was hired as a writer for the film magazine *Fotogramas*, for which he sometimes carried out fake interviews. From 1974 to 1976 he rented a studio apartment from Marguerite Duras. He recounts his Parisian adventures thirty years later in *París no se acaba nunca* (Anagrama, 2004). When he returned to the town where he was born in 1976, Vila-Matas dedicated himself to writing. He also became a columnist for several different Catalan newspapers. For his novel *Montano's Malady*, translated by Jonathan Dunne (New Directions, 2007), he was awarded the prestigious Herralde de Novela Prize in 2002 and the prix Médicis Étranger in 2003.

Bartleby & Co., trans. Jonathan Dunne (New Directions, 2007)

ANNE WEBER was born in Germany in 1964 and lives in Paris. She writes in her mother tongue as well as in French. Among her notable publications are *Chers oiseaux* (Seuil, 2006), *Cerbère* (Seuil, 2004), and *Première personne* (Seuil, 2001). In order to write *Cendres & Métaux* (2006), she set herself up in the dental department of a Swiss company.

Cendres & Métaux (Seuil, 2006)

WEI-WEI, born in the province of Guangxi, China, in 1957, currently lives in England. She is the author of three novels: *La Couleur du bonheur* (Denoël, 1996), *Fleurs de Chine* (L'Aube, 2001), and *Le Yangtsé sacrifié* (Denoël, 1999), all of which were written in French. Her novels, just like her life, consist of a succession of adventures and unexpected endings in which a multitude of characters cross each other's paths. Wei-Wei invites us to discover China—the turmoil and the social, cultural, and political upheavals of her history—through writing filled with lucidity, compassion, and humor.

Une fille Zhuang (L'Aube, 2007)

ALISSA YORK, born in 1970, lives in Canada. She has won many literary prizes for her first novel, *Amours défendues* (Joelle Losfeld, 2007). She also writes short stories.

Effigy (Thomas Dunne Books, 2008)

INDEX

Albahari, David (Silence), 99–100

Ali, Tariq (Laughter), 56–58

Angot, Christine (Faire), 34–35

Arcan, Nelly (Disappointment), 26–28

Ayerdhal (Chaff), 18

Brink, André (Heretic), 43–44

Brisac, Geneviève ([Holy] Russia), 93–94

Byatt, A. S. (The Novel as Web), 76–77

Cañón, James (Mariquita), 65–66

Cendrey, Jean-Yves ([The] Present), 87–89

Chatterjee, Upamanyu (Bildungsroman), 13–14

Chirbes, Rafael (Work), 117–19

Cixous, Hélène (Aletherature), 2–3

Connelly, Karen (Evolution), 32–33

Cooper, Dennis (Signed D. C.), 98–99

Culicchia, Giuseppe (To Last), 55–56

Delaume, Chloé (The Banana Republic of Letters), 11

De Luca, Erri (Island), 53–54

Desplechin, Marie (Echappée), 31–32

Dessaix, Robert (Beauty), 12–13

Ducornet, Rikki (Cunnilingus), 24–25

Duong Thu Huong (Loyalty), 63–64

El Aswany, Alaa (What Is the Novel?), 78–79

El-Daïf, Rachid (I), 46–47

Esterházy, Péter (Words, Words, Words), 116–17

Fagerholm, Monika (Bricoleur), 15–16

Farah, Nuruddin (Identities), 47–48

Fargues, Nicolas (Novice), 80

Fleischer, Alain (Fille), 35–36

Flint, James (Zorby), 122–23

Forest, Philippe (Real), 90–91

Fresán, Rodrigo (The Strolling Mirror), 67–69

Garlini, Alberto (Pathos), 83–84

Groult, Benoîte (Woman), 113–14

Gunn, Kirsty (The Meaning of a Word), 67

Haenel, Yannick (No Why), 73–74

Henric, Jacques (Catin), 17–18

Honoré, Christophe (Breton), 14–15

Hwang Sok-yong (Harmony and Reconciliation), 40–41

Japin, Arthur (The Unreal), 109–11

Jonigk, Thomas (The Depopulated Skies), 100–101

Kaplan, Leslie (The Word *Word*), 114–16

Keret, Etgar (Balagan), 10

Khemiri, Jonas Hassen (Un-), 106–7

Kongoli, Fatos (Suffering), 102–3

Laferrière, Dany (Dream), 29–30

Lang, Luc (Physical), 85–86

Lethem, Jonathan (Furniture), 37

Lustiger, Gila (A Successful Sentence), 95–96

Malinconi, Nicole (The Real), 91–93

McCann, Colum (Anonymity), 4–5

Meek, James (Novel/Life), 77–78

Mendelsohn, Daniel (Unknowable), 108–9

Mercier, Pascal (Wise Imagination), 49

Moody, Rick (Adumbrated), 1–2

Peace, David (Plague), 87

Proulx, Annie (Terroir), 104–5

Rasy, Elisabetta (Shadow), 96–98

Reinhardt, Eric (Cinderella), 19–23

Rosenthal, Olivia (No), 70–73

Saadi, Suhayl (Yusuf), 120–21

Salvayre, Lydie (Paralipomena), 81–83

Shafak, Elif (Nomad), 74–76

Shalev, Zeruya (Amen), 4

Stamm, Peter (Honesty), 45

Tejpal, Tarun J. (India), 49–50

Thirlwell, Adam (Hedonism), 42–43

Trouillot, Lyonel (Available), 7–8

Ulitskaya, Ludmila (Insomnia), 50–53

Van Dis, Adriaan (Lies), 58–62

Verhulst, Dimitri (Awareness of Banality), 8–9

Vilain, Philippe (Autofiction), 5–7

Vila-Matas, Enrique (Discipline), 28

Weber, Anne (Waiting/Attention), 112–13

Wei-Wei (Happiness), 38–39

Ying Chen (Phantom), 84–85

York, Alissa (Creature), 23

CREDITS

.